Diesterweg®

DIESTERWEG READERS

A Trip to London

You're in London. How do you find somewhere to stay? How do you ask someone the way if you get lost? What do you know about British history? What sights* should you visit? How do you order food in a pub? What do you say if you accidentally push someone? *You* decide .... Have a good time!

Lester Vaughan has lived in southern Spain for over ten years. He now teaches English at a private university and writes short stories. He has lived and worked in Europe, the Middle East and South America.

LEVEL FOUR

A Trip to London

LESTER VAUGHAN

Richmond PUBLISHING

Diesterweg®

KEY

Section ■	=	This is where the section starts. eg **Section 10** = Section 10 starts here.
▶	=	Go forward to another section. eg Go to section 10 ▶
◀	=	Go back to another section. eg Go to section 3 ◀
( )	=	The section which you have come from. eg **(48)** = You have come from section 48.
☼	=	The number of points you win. eg Win ☼5 points.
⊘	=	The number of points you lose. eg Lose ⊘5 points.

Introduction

Section 1

1

'Is this your first trip to England?' asks the passenger next to you.

'Yes,' you say, 'I've got a week's holiday from work, so I decided to come to London.'

The aeroplane turns a little and you look through the window. Between the clouds you can see parts of a great city with a wide river running through the middle.

▪■▪

This is the story of your trip to London. In this book you have to make decisions and go to different sections in the book. If you make one decision, you have to go to one section of the book; if you make a different decision, you have to go to a different section of the book.

You win or lose points every day. In some sections you win points if you do or say things correctly. In other sections you lose points if you do or say things incorrectly. Try to get a high score to show that you have had a good holiday.

If you put the book down, don't forget to make a note of your score and section number on a piece of paper.

(There is a glossary at the back of the book to help you with difficult words.)

Points

over 290 points - you have had a marvellous holiday

289 to 235 points - you have had a very good time

234 to 180 points - it has been a good holiday

179 to 80 points - not bad, but not very good either

less than 79 points - better forget this holiday

You start with **100 points.** Write '100' on a piece of paper.

Have a good time in London.

Go to section 10 ▶

2

Section 2

(97)

Answers:

b *the hot air balloon,* invented by the Mongolfier Brothers. They first tried it with animals on 19 September 1783. The balloon was made of paper.

c *electricity.* Electricity from the pieces of metal made the legs move. (Luigi Galvani 1737-98)

d *the yo-yo* originated in the Philippines.

e *sunglasses.*

f *the vacuum cleaner.* Hubert Cecil Booth invented the vacuum cleaner, but he got the idea in London in 1901 from a man who was demonstrating a new wonder machine for cleaning carpets. The machine did not take in air, it blew it out. Hubert told the man to reverse the motor. But the man got angry and said it was not possible.

Win (2) *points for* EACH *correct answer.*

The First Computer?

The mathematician Charles Babbage is considered by many as the inventor of the computer. He designed a mechanical computing machine in the nineteenth century. Unfortunately, the machine was too expensive and difficult to make at the time and it was never finished.

Recently, a team of engineers at the Science Museum built the machine and they found that it worked perfectly. World history might have been very different if Babbage had finished building his machine.

You look at your watch. It is 4.15pm. If you go to the Natural History Museum after 4.30, you do not have to pay. There is a good exhibition about dinosaurs. Do you want to go to the Natural History Museum?

- **Yes.** Go to section 17 ▶
- **No.** Go to section 32 ▶

Section 3

(50)

You walk to Covent Garden. London's main fruit and vegetable market was here until 1974, but now it is a fashionable area full of shops and restaurants. You see a crowd of people watching two clowns*. Covent Garden

Piazza is famous for its street theatre. You watch the clowns for a while, give them some money, then you walk along Neal Street to the British Museum.

Covent Garden Piazza

You go into a large building that looks like a Greek temple (entrance free). You turn left, and you enter the world of the ancient Greeks, Assyrians, Egyptians and Romans. Here you can see the Elgin Marbles, the Rosetta Stone, huge Assyrian statues of animals with human heads, statues of Egyptian kings and lots of mummies.

▪ ■ ▪

Here are some facts about ancient history. One of the facts is false. Which one do you think is false?

a Six thousand life-size soldiers and horses made from terracotta have been found recently in China. They were buried with Shih Hunag Ti, the first Emperor of China, who died in 210BC.

b In ancient Sparta in Greece, boys had to leave their mothers at the age of seven and train to become soldiers. Men and women lived separately for most of their lives.

c In many countries around the Mediterranean, there is a legend* of a fabulous civilization on the lost island of Atlantis. The legend says that the island sank under the sea in one night. Archaeologists have recently found the remains* of a great civilization in the Atlantic Ocean near Portugal which they believe was Atlantis.

d There are millions of mummified cats and other animals buried* in the Egyptian desert.

e When the Anglo-Saxons invaded England in the fifth century AD, they pushed the Celtic Britons into Wales and Brittany in France. Their languages, Welsh and Breton, are very similar.

Go to section 20 ▶

Section 4 (16)

You see a group of American tourists going up some stairs on the right of the building and you follow them. Tom stops suddenly and says, 'Would you mind carrying my things? My leg hurts.' You carry his bag, raincoat, sweater and umbrella. When you think you have come to the end, you turn another corner and there are more stairs. You ask a woman coming down, 'How much further?'

'You're about halfway,' she smiles.

Finally, you get to the Whispering Gallery and you look down at the people below. They are like small insects. The Whispering Gallery is famous for its echo: it is possible to hear someone speaking very quietly from the other side of the dome. You try this with Tom, but unfortunately many people are trying to speak to each other and you hear someone saying, 'Steve, I love you.'

Tom points to some tourists coming down some stairs. 'Oh no!' you say. 'Aren't we at the top yet!'

'*You* go up!' says Tom. 'I'll stay here and look after the bags.'

When you get to the Golden Gallery at the top, you are very tired and it is some time before you can enjoy the beautiful view of London.

Win* 3 *points.

Go to section 36 ▶

5

Section 5

(54)

The correct order is: c, a, f, d, e, b.

Win* 10 *points if you have put* ALL *the sentences in the correct order. *(Write your score on a piece of paper.)*

You think £80 is expensive. What do you say?

- **'I'll take the room.'**
  Go to section 25 ▶

- 'Thank you, I'd like to think about it.' (Then you look for another hotel.)
Go to section 19 ▶

Section 6 (23)

Answers: 2c, 3a, 4e, 5b.

Win 2 points for EACH *correct answer.*

'Shall we go for a trip along the river?' says Tom.

'That's a good idea,' you say.

You go to Westminster Bridge and get on a boat to Hampton Court Palace. When the boat starts, the sun comes out and you can see the Houses of Parliament bathed in sunlight. You sit back and relax while the guide tells you about the places of interest that you pass.

He shows you the building of the British Secret Service with its blue conical roofs, the Peace Pagoda (a temple built by Japanese Buddhist monks) and many other places.

Soon the boat goes under Putney Bridge. This is where the famous boat race* between Oxford and Cambridge Universities takes place in April every year. Each boat has nine people and they have to row* seven kilometres from Putney Bridge to Mortlake. One of the most memorable boat races took place in 1912 when both boats filled with water and sank.

'Isn't this great?' says Tom. 'Look at those beautiful swans.'

Swans were originally introduced into England as food. Most of the swans on the River Thames are royal birds. They belong to the Queen and are protected by

law, but some associations have their own swans and are allowed to catch them and eat them.

Just before Richmond Lock you come to a bird sanctuary. Forty years ago, the Thames was very polluted, but now it is the cleanest industrial river in Europe and it is home to 170 different species of fish.

At the end of a three-hour journey, the boat arrives at Hampton Court, one of the most beautiful palaces in England. It was built by Cardinal Wolsey in 1514. He was later forced to give it to Henry VIII.

When you get off the boat, you see an ice-cream kiosk. Below is your conversation with Tom. Put the sentences in the correct order.

a 'No, I'll get them. It's my turn.'

b 'Yes, I'd love one, but let me pay.'

c 'Oh well, I'll have a large one, please.'

d 'Would you like an ice-cream?'

e 'No, it isn't. You're always paying for things. You paid for the sandwiches on the boat. What do you want?'

Go to section 28 ▶

Section 7 (70)

Answers: apples and pears - stairs; boat race - face; brown bread - dead; whistle and flute - suit.

Win 2 points for EACH correct answer.

You get a bus to the centre of London and get off at Trafalgar Square. Above you on a high column is the statue of the very famous Admiral Nelson who lost an eye and an arm in battle. His ships beat Napoleon's ships at the Battle of Trafalgar in 1805, but Nelson died in the battle. (The Duke of Wellington beat Napoleon on land at the Battle of Waterloo in 1815. However, he did not die in battle, and he later became a politician, so his statue is not as big).

You wait near one of the lions for 15 minutes, but Tom does not come and you start to worry. Finally, 30 minutes later, you see his angry face appearing from behind another lion.

You argue with Tom. Put the sentences in the correct order.

Example: 1c

a 'I was here. Where were you?'
b 'Well, you were in front of the wrong lion!'
c 'I've been waiting for you for nearly an hour!'
d 'In front of that lion where we were supposed to meet.'
e 'Well, I've been waiting for *you* for nearly an hour! Where were you, then?'

Now go to section 24 ▶

8

Section 8

(11) (38)

You take a train to Vauxhall Station. When you are on the train, you see some men in the distance, dressed in white, playing a game of cricket. 'No one's moving!' you say to Tom. Then a man runs and throws a ball at another man.

'It's not surprising they don't move much. It takes a long time to play a game of cricket,' says Tom. 'We play it a lot in Australia. I love it.'

Do you want to know some interesting facts about cricket?

- **Yes.** Go to section 13 ▶
- **No.** Go to section 26 ▶

9

Section 9

(60)

She says a lot of things you do not understand and then hits you with her cycling bag.

Lose (5) *points.*

The nurse puts a plaster on your face and you take a taxi home.

Go to section 15 ▶

10

Section 10

(1)

It is Sunday. You have just arrived at Heathrow Airport near London. Your plane was delayed and it is now nine o'clock in the evening. You do not have the address of a hotel and there is a long queue at

Section 7 (70)

Answers: apples and pears - stairs; boat race - face; brown bread - dead; whistle and flute - suit.

Win (2) *points for* EACH *correct answer.*

You get a bus to the centre of London and get off at Trafalgar Square. Above you on a high column is the statue of the very famous Admiral Nelson who lost an eye and an arm in battle. His ships beat Napoleon's ships at the Battle of Trafalgar in 1805, but Nelson died in the battle. (The Duke of Wellington beat Napoleon on land at the Battle of Waterloo in 1815. However, he did not die in battle, and he later became a politician, so his statue is not as big).

You wait near one of the lions for 15 minutes, but Tom does not come and you start to worry. Finally, 30 minutes later, you see his angry face appearing from behind another lion.

You argue with Tom. Put the sentences in the correct order.

Example: 1c

a 'I was here. Where were you?'

b 'Well, you were in front of the wrong lion!'

c 'I've been waiting for you for nearly an hour!'

d 'In front of that lion where we were supposed to meet.'

e 'Well, I've been waiting for *you* for nearly an hour! Where were you, then?'

Now go to section 24 ▶

8 Section 8 (11) (38)

You take a train to Vauxhall Station. When you are on the train, you see some men in the distance, dressed in white, playing a game of cricket. 'No one's moving!' you say to Tom. Then a man runs and throws a ball at another man.

'It's not surprising they don't move much. It takes a long time to play a game of cricket,' says Tom. 'We play it a lot in Australia. I love it.'

Do you want to know some interesting facts about cricket?

- **Yes.** Go to section 13 ▶
- **No.** Go to section 26 ▶

9 Section 9 (60)

She says a lot of things you do not understand and then hits you with her cycling bag.

Lose 5 points.

The nurse puts a plaster on your face and you take a taxi home.

Go to section 15 ▶

10 Section 10 (1)

It is Sunday. You have just arrived at Heathrow Airport near London. Your plane was delayed and it is now nine o'clock in the evening. You do not have the address of a hotel and there is a long queue at the tourist information desk. You decide to go to the centre of London and find a place to sleep.

What do you do?

- **Take a taxi.**
  Go to section 21 ▶

- **Go by underground.**
  Go to section 30 ▶

(If you want to take a taxi, go to section 21.)
(If you want to go by underground train, go to section 30.)

Section 11 (28)

A young keeper hears you and shouts, 'Stay there! I'll come and get you.' You wait for five minutes, but he does not appear. 'Where are you?' he shouts.

'Here!' you shout. You hear his voice on the other side of the hedge, but he cannot find you. The French girl starts crying again.

Finally, an older keeper comes and shows you the way out. You feel so happy to be still alive that you spend too much money on lunch at Hampton Court restaurant.

Go to section 8 ◀

12

Section 12 (15)

One of these facts is false. Which one do you think is false?

a When people used to carry swords, it was safer to pass someone on the left. If the person you were passing tried to attack you, you could more easily defend yourself on your right side (if you were right-handed).

b Two thousand years ago, Julius Caesar ordered everyone in the Roman Empire to drive on the left.

c Before 1800, most countries in Europe drove on the left. It was Napoleon Bonaparte who ordered everyone to drive on the right.

d Britain is now the only country in the world where people drive on the left.

Go to section 18 ▶

13

Section 13 (8)

Here are some facts about cricket.

- At one time, it was considered an essential part of every Englishman's education to learn how to play cricket - more important than learning maths or history.
- A game of cricket can take five days. (Less important matches are played in one day.)
- The worst cricket team in England were the Utopers XI from University College, Oxford. They played for 33 years before they won a game.

People think the rules of cricket are very complicated, but really they are quite easy. Read this description.

The Rules of Cricket

There are two teams and 11 players in each team. One team is in and the other is out. The team that is in has only two players in at one time, and the team that is out has all of its players on the field. The team that is out has to get a player who is in out, in which case the player who is out goes in the pavilion, and the next player comes out and is now in. If there is only one player left on the field, although he is not out, he has to go in. Then the team that is out is in, and the team that is now out has to get the team that is now in out.

(The real rules of cricket are very complicated and take a long time to learn.)

Go to section 26 ▶

Section 14 (34)

You say, 'I'll have a hamburger and chips.'

'You're not very adventurous, are you?' says Tom.

Go to section 22 ▶

Section 15 (9) (37)

You tell the taxi driver about the accident. 'That often happens in London,' he says. 'Foreigners look the wrong way when they cross the road. They forget we drive on the left.'

Do you want to know why the British drive on the left?

- **Yes.** Go to section 12 ◀|
- **No.** Go to section 23 |▶

16

Section 16 (50)

You get off the bus and, in front of you, you see the famous dome* of St Paul's Cathedral. It is 111 metres high. You pay and go inside. Above you is the impressive dome decorated with paintings of the life of St Paul.

St Paul's Cathedral was designed by Sir Christopher Wren and took 35 years to complete (1675-1710). While it was being built, a new expression became popular - 'as slow as St Paul's

Do you want to go up to the top of the dome?

Cathedral'. In fact cathedrals usually take at least a hundred years to build, and Sir Christopher Wren was one of the few architects of cathedrals to see his work finished. Sir Christopher Wren designed 50 more churches, although his only formal training in architecture was a six-month period in Paris. He was really an astronomer and a scientist, and he invented many things. He died at the age of 91.

Here are some more facts about St Paul's Cathedral.

- In Roman times there was a temple to the Goddess Diana on this site.
- Alexander Fleming, the Duke of Wellington and many other famous people are buried here.
- Admiral Nelson's body is buried in the centre of St Paul's Cathedral – it is preserved in brandy.
- Prince Charles and Lady Diana were married here.

Do you want to go up to the top of the dome?

- Yes.
  Go to section 4 ◀|
- No.
  Go to section 36 |▶

Section 17 (2)

You walk to the end of Exhibition Road and turn right towards the beautiful neo-romanesque building of the Natural History Museum.

You go in. In front of you there is a skeleton of an enormous dinosaur. You turn left into the Dinosaur Gallery. At the end of the gallery there are models of a group of small dinosaurs attacking a larger one. They are the same size as real dinosaurs; they move and look very real.

Here are some facts about dinosaurs. *One* of the facts is false. Which one do you think is false?

a Three thousand fossilized dinosaur eggs have been found buried on an ancient beach in Lerida, Spain.

b Many dinosaurs made nests for their eggs and looked after their young in the same way that birds do today.

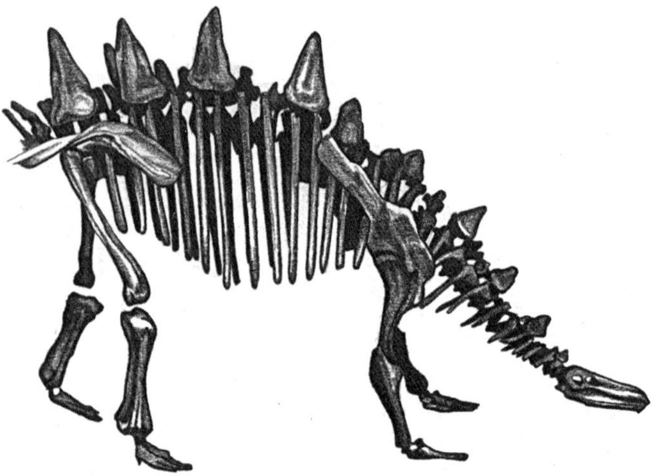

c No one knows why the dinosaurs became extinct. Many scientists think it was because a large meteorite hit the earth. Others think it was because the plants and the climate changed.

d Some dinosaurs did not become completely extinct - they evolved and became birds.

e Humans hunted small dinosaurs and lived in caves to escape being eaten by them.

Go to section 29 ▶

Section 18 (12)

18

Answer: d is false. India, Japan and other countries drive on the left.

Win 5 *points if you answered correctly.*

Go to section 23 ▶

Section 19 (5)

19

You walk along the dark streets, but you cannot see a hotel. It is raining heavily. Your suitcase is completely wet and some water is going down the back of your neck.

Lose 5 *points. (Write down your score.)*

Finally, you see a sign. It says 'Tudor Hotel'. You go in and ask the receptionist the price of a room. She says £80. You decide to stay.

Go to section 25 ▶

Section 20 (3)

20

Answer: c is false, but archaeologists *have* found the remains of a great civilization on the Island of Thira in south-eastern Greece. It was destroyed by a volcano 3,500 years ago. Many archaeologists think that this was how the legend of Atlantis originated.

Win 10 *points if you answered correctly.*

You go to the section of Greek and Roman antiquities and see the Elgin Marbles. These were taken from the

A section of the frieze from the Parthenon, now in the British Museum

Parthenon in Athens in Greece at the beginning of the nineteenth century by the Englishman, Lord Elgin. Part of the Temple of Apollo at Bassae in Greece is in the same section. Then you see the Egyptian collection (some of which was 'taken' from Napoleon, who had 'taken' it from the Egyptians). The British Museum has the largest collection of Egyptian antiquities in the world.

Tom spends a long time in the Manuscript Room, looking at old books and manuscripts. He shows you the famous Magna Carta, a document written in 1215. King John was forced to sign the Magna Carta by his nobles. By signing it, he agreed to give political rights to the nobles and people of England.

After you have seen a few more galleries, you sit down on a seat and say to Tom, 'I can't walk any more.' The British Museum is too big to see in one visit.

Go back to section 50 ▶

Section 21 (10)

You walk into the cool night air. After waiting for a short time in a queue, you get into a large black London taxi. There is plenty of space inside: a London taxi can carry four people in the back.

You say, 'Could you take me to a hotel in the centre of London, please?'

'What kind of hotel do you want?' asks the taxi driver. 'Three-star, two-star, bed and breakfast?'

'What's a bed and breakfast?' you ask.

'It's a kind of small family hotel, and breakfast is included in the price.'

'Is it cheap?' you ask.

'Yes, usually. I always stay at bed and breakfasts when I travel. They're more friendly than normal hotels.'

What do you do?

- **Go to a bed and breakfast.**
  Go to section 35 ▶

- **Go to a two-star hotel.**
  Go to section 51 ▶

Section 22

(14) (39)

While you are eating, you hear a bell ring. It is from the Houses of Parliament, which are near. The bell is to tell any Members of Parliament who are in the pub that it is time to vote.

After lunch, you walk to Big Ben, the famous clock tower next to the Houses of Parliament. You pass the statue of Queen Boadicea, the Celtic queen who destroyed London in AD61, and walk along Westminster Bridge. From Westminster Bridge you have a good view of the Houses of Parliament. The original Parliament buildings were destroyed by fire in 1834. The buildings you see today were built between 1839 and 1848 in the neo-Gothic style.

You walk back to Parliament Square. It is a very hot day and you find it difficult to carry your coat, sweater and umbrella. Opposite the Houses of Parliament is Westminster Abbey, the famous church where the kings and queens of England are crowned.

'Where would you like to go?' you ask Tom.

'I don't mind,' he says.

Which place do you visit?

- **The Houses of Parliament.**
  Go to section 33 ▶
- **Westminster Abbey.**
  Go to section 74 ▶

Section 23

(15) (18)

The taxi takes you to the bed and breakfast.

▪ ■ ▪

It is Friday - your last full day in London. You are leaving tomorrow morning.

Mrs Lovedale brings your breakfast. 'It's going to be another hot day!' she says sadly. You are sitting next to two Japanese girls at the breakfast table. They say they are travelling around Europe on a Euro-rail Pass. (With this card you can go anywhere in Europe by train for a month if you are under 26 years old.) They spend most of their time in trains. They are going to see London today and Scotland tomorrow.

You meet Tom at Piccadilly Circus. 'Why are you wearing a bandage?' he asks when he sees you. You tell him what happened last night and he laughs. You do not think it is funny.

Here are some jokes about doctors. Try to find the right ending for each beginning.

Example: **1d**

Beginnings

1 Patient: I've only got 55 seconds to live.
2 Patient: How long can a person live without a brain?
3 Patient: I've just eaten a whole sheep.
Doctor: How do you feel?
4 Doctor: Do you have difficulty making decisions?
5 Patient: Every night I dream I'm a comedian.

Endings

a Patient: Very baaa-aaa-aad.
b Doctor: You must be joking.
c Doctor: I don't know. How old are you?
d Doctor: Just a minute!
e Patient: Well, yes and no.

Go to section 6 ◀|

Section 24 (7)

The correct order is: c, e, a, d, b.

Win 10 points if ALL the sentences are in the correct order.

Remember, this is England and you should try to be calm. You do not talk to each other for some time.

You go under Admiralty Arch and you come to a red road called the Mall. At the end of the road you can see Buckingham Palace. You cross the road and go into St James's Park, one of the prettiest parks in London. It is very nice. The sun is warm, the park is very green, there are birds, ducks and tourists everywhere. 'Look, there's a pelican,' says Tom. 'I can't believe we're in the centre of London.' The park is a nature reserve and there are over 30 different varieties of bird in the park.

There is a restaurant by the lake with chairs outside. It is a good place to have a nice cup of tea while Tom looks at the birds. You have your tea English style: a lot of water and a little milk. It tastes very good.

Do you want to know more about tea?

- **Yes.** Go to section 27 ▶
- **No.** Go to section 34 ▶

Section 25

(5) (19)

The porter takes you to your room. It is large and comfortable. But the hotel is too expensive and you have spent too much money.

Lose (10) *points. (Write down your score.)*

It is Monday morning. After breakfast, you pay the bill and leave the hotel. You have to find a cheaper place. You go to the tourist information office at Victoria Station and they give you the address of a bed and breakfast. A bed and breakfast is a small family hotel - often a large house. They are usually cheap, clean and friendly. You take a taxi there.

The taxi stops at a large Victorian house with a sign in the window: 'Lovedales' Bed and Breakfast - Rooms Vacant'. You ring* the bell* and the door is opened by a thin man in a large blue sweater, holding

a small dog. You ask, 'Have you got a single room?'

He smiles and says, 'Yes, come this way.'

He shows you a clean room with a television, thick red carpet and blue curtains. On the table there is an electric kettle for making coffee or tea. You decide to spend the week there. It will cost £125 for five nights, including breakfast. You fall on the bed and smile.

Go to section 40 ▶

Section 26 (8) (13)

'I forgot to tell you,' says Tom, while you are walking to the underground station. 'My friend's got a friend who knows someone who's having a party tonight, and she said we could go. We might meet some English people.'

'Oh, that sounds good,' you say.

'It's a fancy dress party,' says Tom.

'A fancy dress party!?' you say.

'Yes, you know, you have to wear funny clothes like Dracula or Batman,' says Tom.

'But where are we going to get the costumes?'

'My friend gave me the address of a shop where you can hire costumes. It's open till nine on Friday evenings, so we can go there after dinner.'

You take the underground back to Central London. You have an early dinner at a Thai restaurant and then take the underground to the fancy dress shop.

You walk down some narrow streets until you find an old shop on the corner. You go in and an old lady says, 'Can I help you?'

Below is your conversation with the lady. Use these words to complete the dialogue:

size take about fit suit changing

You: I'm looking for a vampire costume.
Lady: I'm afraid we haven't got any vampire costumes left. We've had a lot of customers today.
You: How (a)... a pirate?
Lady: Sorry, in your size we've only got an angel costume.

You: I don't think an angel costume would (b)... me.
Lady: Oh, I don't know. Try it on.
You: Where is the (c)... room?
Lady: Over there.
(You put the costume on and come back. The costume touches the floor.)
Lady: Perfect.
You: I don't agree. It doesn't (d)... me. It's too long and the wings are a bit big. Have you got a smaller (e)...?
Lady: I'll have a look. Here you are.
(You try it on and decide to hire it.)
You: I'll (f)... it.

Go to section 76 ▶

27

Section 27 (24)

Here are some facts about tea.

- Half the world's population drinks tea.
- Tea was drunk by the Chinese over 3,000 years ago.
- Hot water kills bacteria, and it is thought that people began drinking hot water because it was safer. Later, they thought of flavouring the hot water with tea leaves.
- In Tibet and China tea was used as a form of money for nearly 1,000 years.
- New York was the first place in the West where tea was tried. However, the New Yorkers did not know how to make it properly and ate the tea leaves with bread and butter.

Go to section 34 ▶

Section 26

(8) (13)

'I forgot to tell you,' says Tom, while you are walking to the underground station. 'My friend's got a friend who knows someone who's having a party tonight, and she said we could go. We might meet some English people.'

'Oh, that sounds good,' you say.

'It's a fancy dress party,' says Tom.

'A fancy dress party!?' you say.

'Yes, you know, you have to wear funny clothes like Dracula or Batman,' says Tom.

'But where are we going to get the costumes?'

'My friend gave me the address of a shop where you can hire costumes. It's open till nine on Friday evenings, so we can go there after dinner.'

You take the underground back to Central London. You have an early dinner at a Thai restaurant and then take the underground to the fancy dress shop.

You walk down some narrow streets until you find an old shop on the corner. You go in and an old lady says, 'Can I help you?'

Below is your conversation with the lady. Use these words to complete the dialogue:

size take about fit suit changing

You: I'm looking for a vampire costume.

Lady: I'm afraid we haven't got any vampire costumes left. We've had a lot of customers today.

You: How (a)... a pirate?

Lady: Sorry, in your size we've only got an angel costume.

You: I don't think an angel costume would (b)... me.
Lady: Oh, I don't know. Try it on.
You: Where is the (c)... room?
Lady: Over there.
(You put the costume on and come back. The costume touches the floor.)
Lady: Perfect.
You: I don't agree. It doesn't (d)... me. It's too long and the wings are a bit big. Have you got a smaller (e)...?
Lady: I'll have a look. Here you are.
(You try it on and decide to hire it.)
You: I'll (f)... it.

Go to section 76 ▶

27

Section 27 (24)

Here are some facts about tea.

- Half the world's population drinks tea.
- Tea was drunk by the Chinese over 3,000 years ago.
- Hot water kills bacteria, and it is thought that people began drinking hot water because it was safer. Later, they thought of flavouring the hot water with tea leaves.
- In Tibet and China tea was used as a form of money for nearly 1,000 years.
- New York was the first place in the West where tea was tried. However, the New Yorkers did not know how to make it properly and ate the tea leaves with bread and butter.

Go to section 34 ▶

Section 28 (6)

The correct order is: d, b, a, e, c.

Win 10 points if ALL *the sentences are in the correct order.*

You get a ticket and go down a long road, through the beautiful Great Gatehouse to the Clock Court where you can see the Astronomical Clock built in the time of King Henry VIII. You go up some stairs to Henry VIII's State Apartments and see the magnificent sixteenth-century Great Hall and Chapel Royal. A guide tells you about the Haunted Gallery where Queen Catherine Howard (Henry VIII's fifth wife) is said to appear on the anniversary of her death. Many guides and cleaners have left their jobs at Hampton Court because they think they have seen ghosts.

The Astronomical Clock was built for Henry VIII.

You go to back to the Clock Court and wait for a guide to show you the State Apartments. A guide wearing seventeenth-century dress takes you up the King's Staircase to the King's Guard Room where you can see 3,000 guns on the walls. In the Wolsey Rooms, you have a beautiful view of the Privy Gardens that have recently been restored. The guide tells you that in the time of King William of Orange only a few privileged people were allowed into the gardens.

The guide is very interested in the eating habits of that period. She tells you that at mealtimes the King was given a lot of different dishes to choose from. After the King had eaten what he wanted, the courtiers came into the room and ate the rest of the food. She tells you that the King ate a lot of vegetables and fruit, but his doctors thought that this food was not healthy and they tried to make him have only meat, sugar and wine.

You visit the sixteenth-century Tudor kitchens and then you go out to the magnificent Fountain Garden. You walk past the Tudor Tennis Courts and you come to the famous Hampton Court Maze.

Tom says, 'Come on, let's go in,' and you enter the maze. Soon you meet a man sitting on a bench with his head between his hands. He says that he has been trying to find the way out for over an hour. 'Follow me!' says Tom. 'I know how to get out.' And you and the man follow Tom. Ten minutes later, you come back to the same bench. This time they follow you. You meet a French girl who has lost her friends and she follows you, too. Sometimes the girl can hear her friends talking on the other side of the hedge, and you meet some people that you have passed before, but soon you come back to the same bench. This time the man sits on the bench saying, 'I'm too tired to go on. I'll just wait until you come back again.' Five minutes later, you are back in the same place. The French girl starts crying.

What do you do?

- **Try to find the way out again.**
  Go to section 38 ▶
- **Call the keeper (the man who looks after the maze).**
  Go to section 11 ◀

Section 29 (17)

Answer: e is false. There were no humans when dinosaurs lived on the earth.

Win 10 *points if you answered correctly.*

You go into the Whale* Hall, where you can see a model of a blue whale, the largest whale in the world. It is the same size as a real whale and it fills the hall.

There are many more exciting exhibits: minerals, fish, birds, the evolution of man, and the Earth Galleries, where you can travel through the centre of the earth, discover how the earth was formed and experience an earthquake*. But it is nearly six o'clock now. The museum is closing and you have to leave.

Go to section 32 ▶

Section 30 (10)

You go down long tunnels, following the signs for the underground. You buy a ticket and wait eight minutes for a train. There are people from all around the world on the train: Chinese, Africans, a few Americans, a few English....

You have saved a lot of money coming by underground. Heathrow is a long way from the centre of London. A taxi costs about £35 and the underground costs £4.

Win 5 *points. (You now have 100 + 5 = 105 points. Write '105' on a piece of paper.)*

Forty minutes later, you arrive at Gloucester Road Underground Station. The machine takes your ticket and you go out of the station into the rain. It is now 10pm. Some people pass quickly, holding umbrellas, but they soon disappear into the night. You walk and walk in the rain. Finally, you see a sign which says, 'Crescent Hotel'.

Go to section 54 ▶

Section 31 (50)

You get off the bus at Marble Arch. Marble Arch is a large white triumphal arch near Hyde Park. It was originally the entrance to Buckingham Palace, but it was too small so they moved it.

You walk to Speaker's Corner (in the north-east corner of Hyde Park). You see a man standing on a box, speaking loudly to a few people about changing the British political system. There are not many people today because it is Tuesday. But on Sundays there are usually several people standing on boxes, trying to convince sceptical audiences of their ideas.

People come here to speak about anything they think is important. At one time this was the only place in England where people could say what they wanted without fear of arrest. You are still free to say what you

You can say whatever you like at Speaker's Corner.

want here. In 1987, for example, the book *Spycatcher* was prohibited in Britain. Some Members of Parliament read the book to a group of spectators at Speaker's Corner. They were not arrested.

You walk through Hyde Park. It is green for as far as the eye can see. There are some people riding horses and a military band is playing in the distance. When you get to the Serpentine Lake, Tom says, 'Let's hire* a boat.' He pays the man and you both get into a boat. Tom lies down in the front of the boat and puts his hands behind his head. You start rowing. You really enjoy being in the boat, but after 15 minutes you do not find rowing so interesting. Tom says sleepily, 'It's nice to be in a boat on such a lovely day.'

What do you say to Tom?

- **'Would you be so kind as to row now? I'm tired.'**
  Go to section 53 ▶
- **'Would you mind rowing for a bit? I'm tired.'**
  Go to section 65 ▶

Section 32 (2) (29)

'Let's go to a park,' says Tom.

You walk past the Victoria and Albert Museum to the Royal Albert Hall. In front of the Albert Hall you can see the large Albert Memorial. 'Who was this Albert guy?' asks Tom. Your guidebook tells you that this area is called Albertopolis, and that Prince Albert was Queen Victoria's husband. He was very interested in culture and education.

You go into Kensington Gardens. In Victorian

times, people could not enter if they were not well dressed. Now you can wear anything.

You walk to Kensington Palace where Diana, Princess of Wales, lived. You hear the sound of electric motors and go to the pond where some old men are controlling model boats with radios. Suddenly one boat hits another and two men start shouting at each other.

'I think what I like most about London are the parks,' says Tom and he lies down on the grass.

Kensington Roof Gardens

London is famous for its parks and gardens, but not many people know that not far from Kensington Gardens are the Kensington Roof Gardens – the largest roof gardens in Europe. These pretty gardens are on the top of a department-store building (entrance in Derry Street). Here you can find a small lake with ducks* and flamingos, and even an imitation Spanish convent and palm trees.

A few minutes later, the sun goes in and there are black clouds above you. 'Oh no!' says Tom. 'It's going to rain.' Soon it is raining and neither of you has brought your umbrella or raincoat. You run out of the park and find a café. Tom sneezes*.

What do you say?

- **'Bless you.'**
  Go to section 42 ▶
- **'Jesus.'**
  Go to section 55 ▶

Section 33

(22)

You walk to the Houses of Parliament and stand in a queue. The Houses of Parliament are divided into two principal parts: the House of Lords and the House of Commons (which has the real power). You are lucky - today you can enter the House of Commons.

Ten thousand people work in the Houses of Parliament. It is like a small town inside with a post office, police station, hairdresser, travel agent, 14 bars and restaurants, and a chess room (the only game allowed here).

The queue moves quickly and you go into St Steven's Hall which has a high Gothic ceiling* and looks like the interior of a church. Then you go up a lot of stairs to the Public Gallery of the Chamber* of House of Commons.

MPs debate in the House of Commons.

It is surprisingly small with green leather benches. In the middle sits the Speaker who directs the debates. A Member of Parliament (MP) is standing and saying something about libraries in England. There are only three other MPs in the chamber. When the MP finishes, he leaves the chamber and another MP stands up and speaks.

Tom says that the debate is very boring and you leave.

Here are some facts about the Houses of Parliament. One of them is false. Which one?

a There are 635 Members of Parliament and only enough seats for 450 people in the Chamber of the House of Commons.

b The Queen cannot enter the Chamber of the House of Commons.

c A man called Guy Fawkes tried to blow up Parliament in 1605, but he was caught. Every year, on 5 November, the English celebrate this with fireworks*.

d The English electoral system and the Spanish electoral system are similar.

e There is a second chamber called the Chamber of the House of Lords. The Lords are not elected. Most of them inherit their seat from their father or they are chosen by the Prime Minister.

Go to section 46 ▶

Section 34 (24)

You leave the restaurant and walk through the park until you come to an open-air concert of classical music. Eight women are playing Vivaldi. Some people are listening, others are sleeping in chairs.

In the distance you hear the sound of military music. Tom says, 'Come on!' and you walk quickly towards Buckingham Palace. There are soldiers in red uniforms and large black hats going around the Victoria Monument.

You cross the road and try to see what is happening in front of Buckingham Palace, but there are too many tourists. Sometimes you see a red uniform, sometimes a sword shines in the sun. There is a policeman on a horse who is joking with the tourists. Tom asks the policeman, 'What's happening?'

'It's the changing of the guard,' says the policeman. 'They'll be coming out in a minute.' The band plays Beatles' music for a while. Then the gates open and a soldier with a dog leaves the palace followed by a lot more soldiers. The crowd disappears and you see a few guards with guns in front of the palace.

You try to see what is happening in front of Buckingham Palace.

The royal flag is up which means the Queen is at home. Buckingham Palace is open to visitors in August and September when the Queen is on holiday.

You walk along Birdcage Walk beside St James's Park. 'Let's have a pub lunch,' says Tom. You find a pub and go in. Tom looks at the menu. 'They've got roast beef* and Yorkshire pudding,' he says. 'You can't go back to your country without trying roast beef and Yorkshire pudding. It's what everybody eats here at Sunday lunchtime.'

What do you have?

- **Roast beef and Yorkshire pudding.**
  Go to section 39 ▶
- **Hamburger and chips.**
  Go to section 14 ◀

Section 35

(21)

Thirty minutes later, the taxi drives into a quiet street and you see a large Victorian house with the

sign, 'Lovedales' Bed and Breakfast - Rooms Vacant'.

'That's £36,' says the taxi driver. You give him a £4 tip*. (It's normal to tip taxi drivers about 10%.) You feel happy that you have found a hotel. The taxi driver looks very happy, too. Heathrow Airport is a long way from the centre of London, and the trip was quite expensive. By underground it is about £4.

Lose* (5) *points. *(You now have 100 - 5 = 95 points. Write '95' on a piece of paper.)*

You ring* the bell*, and the door is opened by a thin man in a large red sweater. He is holding a cat. You ask, 'Have you got a single room?' He smiles and says, 'Yes, come this way.'

The room is clean, with a television, thick red carpet and green curtains. On the table there is an electric kettle for making coffee or tea.

Look at your conversation with Mr Lovedale. Put the sentences in the correct order.

Example: **1c**

a 'Yes. An evening meal is £6.'
b 'That's OK. I don't mind. How much is it?'
c 'Has it got a bathroom?'
d 'It's £25 a night. How long would you like to stay?'
e 'I'll take the room.'
f 'I'm afraid not. The bathroom's at the end of the hall.'
g 'Six nights. Is breakfast included in the price?'

Go to section 47 ▶

Section 36

(4) (16)

Pocahontas and John Smith

Outside Mary-le-Bow Church, not far from St Paul's Cathedral, there is a statue of Captain John Smith (1580-1631). This statue is an exact copy of one in Jamestown, USA.

John Smith was an adventurer and soldier who travelled to North America in 1607 to establish a colony. In America, John Smith met the Indian girl, Pocahontas. Two years later, John Smith came back to England and began writing books about his travels.

In 1616, Pocahontas came to London and met John Smith again. She met the King and Queen of England and many important people. But a year later, when she was going back to America, Pocahontas died. She was buried just outside London at St George's Church, Gravesend, and there is a statue of her not far from the church. Descendants of Pocahontas still live in Jamestown, USA.

Go back to section 50 and visit another place ▶

Section 37

(60)

The cyclist says yes and you take her home in the taxi. When she gets out of the taxi, you say to her, 'Well, it's been nice meeting you. Goodbye.' She does not say anything.

Go to section 15 ◀

38 Section 38

(28)

This time you are lucky. After only five minutes, you find the way out of the maze. The French girl kisses you, and the man buys you a cup of tea and a cake at the Hampton Court tearoom.

Win 3 points.

Go to section 8

39 Section 39

(34)

The barman gives you the roast beef and Yorkshire pudding. The beef is cut thin and cooked in the oven* with potatoes and Yorkshire pudding. Yorkshire pudding is made from milk, eggs and flour*. It is all served on the same plate with boiled vegetables. Gravy is a meat sauce* which you pour over the meat and vegetables.

Go to section 22

40 Section 40

(25) (47)

You look through the window. People are walking along the street, fighting with their umbrellas. It is windy and rainy, not a good day for going to a park or for a trip on the river.

You look at your guidebook and decide to visit the Tower of London, the nine hundred-year-old castle where many famous people were executed. But first you have to buy an umbrella.

You ask Mrs Lovedale, 'Is there a shop near here

where I can buy an umbrella?'

'At the end of the street,' says Mrs Lovedale.

'Is this normal weather for July?' you ask.

'There isn't normal weather in England in summer: sometimes it rains, and sometimes it's sunny,' says Mrs Lovedale. 'Last summer it was so hot I didn't know what to do.'

You leave the hotel and run to the shop. You see the umbrella you want behind the assistant.

What do you say to the assistant?

- **'Can I have that umbrella, please?'**
  Go to section 72 ▶
- **'Give me that umbrella, please.'**
  Go to section 86 ▶

Section 41

(50)

On the Victoria Embankment next to the River Thames, there is a large Egyptian obelisk called Cleopatra's Needle. Although it is called Cleopatra's Needle, it was made for King Thothmes III in about 1480BC. Cleopatra was not born until about 69BC.

In 1877, a special container was made for the 160-tonne obelisk and it was transported from Egypt to London. On the way to

England, the container nearly sank* in a storm and six sailors* lost their lives. Then the container was lost at sea for a time until a British ship found it. The obelisk finally arrived in London in 1878.

Under the obelisk was placed a time capsule - a special box for future generations to find. It contained many articles of the time, including some coins*, some newspapers, a railway guide and pictures of twelve of the most beautiful women of the day.

There are similar Egyptian obelisks in Paris and New York.

Go back to section 50 and visit another place ▶

42

Section 42 (32)

Correct. Tom sneezes again. Tom has got a wet copy of *Time Out*.

Time Out is a magazine which tells you what is happening in London at the moment. It gives information about films, music, theatre, dance, art, shopping, food and so on. Look at these extracts from *Time Out*:

ROCK, REGGAE & SOUL

★Eddy Sanders Band + Tomcats Supercharged rock from Sanders, and Tomcats' existential guitar dementia. The Blockhouse, W1. 8.30pm. £5.

CLASSICAL

★BBC Henry Wood Promenade Concerts All tickets are bookable on 0171-589 8212.Wednesday, July 19 London Symphony Orchestra, conducted by David Ramsden, playing Strauss *Till Euslenspiegel*, Tchaikovsky Violin Concerto with Boris Belkin, Rachmaninov Symphonic Dances, 8pm, £5-£20.

Where would you like to go?

- **To the rock concert.**
  Go to section 61 ▶
- **To the classical music concert.**
  Go to section 75 ▶

Section 43

(93) (103)

Mr Lovedale looks worried. 'You'll never catch Joey now. My wife loves that bird,' he says. 'She'll be upset for a week about this.'

'Maybe I can buy another one,' you say.

'Good idea,' says Mr Lovedale. 'There's a pet shop* not far from here. Go straight on until the end of the road, then turn left. Go on for about 100 yards* and you'll come to a roundabout. Go round the roundabout and take the third turning on the left. Go over a bridge, past a church. Go straight across the traffic lights and follow the road until the end.

Then turn left and it's on the left. You can't miss it. Hurry! She'll be back soon.'

You go and get the bird cage.

Look at the map and follow Mr Lovedale's directions. Are you at 49, 58 or 68?

If you are at 49, go to section 49 ▶

If you are at 58, go to section 58 ▶

If you are at 68, go to section 68 ▶

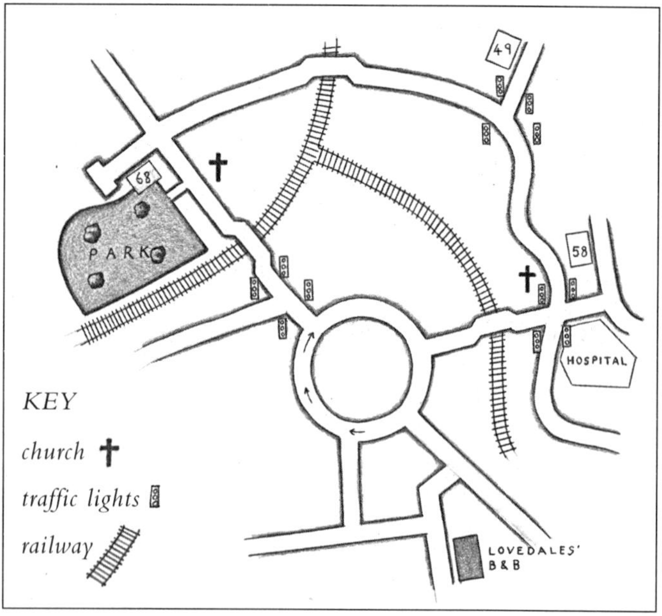

44

Section 44 (105)

The correct order is: c, f, d, a, e, b.

Win 10 *points if* ALL *the sentences are in the correct order.*

When you are speaking to the woman, a man says to you angrily, 'Would you mind being quiet? I can't hear!'

You enjoy the show very much. At the end, when the rats are all friends again, you are singing with the rest of the audience.

You decide to catch a taxi home. You wait on the corner of the street until a free taxi comes. Then you walk into the road and put your hand out. The next moment you are lying on the road with a bicycle on top of you. You did not look right when you were crossing the road and a cyclist hit you.

The taxi takes you and the cyclist to hospital.

Look at your conversation with the doctor below. Put the sentences in the correct order.

a 'Ow! That hurt!'
b 'What's the matter?'
c 'Sorry. I don't think it's anything serious. We'll take an X-ray and the nurse will put a bandage on it.'
d 'Let me have a look.'
e 'I've hurt my hand. A bicycle hit it.'

Now go to section 60 ▶

Section 45 (100)

Answers: b Superman, c policewoman, d pirate, e clown, f Dracula.

Win **2** *points for* EACH *correct answer.*

It is getting very late now. Tom starts talking to the policewoman.

'Hello,' he says.

'Who's the owner of this house?' asks the policewoman.

'I think it's Cleopatra,' says Tom. 'That's a really good costume. You look like a real policewoman. You know, I really hate the police.' He gives her his mask, and takes her hat and puts it on his head.

'Give that back to me or I'll have to arrest you!' says the policewoman.

'Oh, I'm going to be arrested! You speak like a real policewoman, too,' says Tom, and he takes her whistle and blows it.

'I *am* a real policewoman,' says the woman.

'Sorry,' says Tom,' I didn't catch what you said.'

'I said I *AM* a real policewoman!'

'What's the matter?' asks Cleopatra.

'We've had complaints from the neighbours about the noise,' says the policewoman. 'They said there were strange things happening here. I want the music turned off now! And *YOU*,' she points at Tom, 'can come with us!' She takes Tom out of the house.

'Don't take him!' you shout. 'He was only joking. He's not dangerous - he's just a bit silly at times, that's all!'

Through the window, you can see a gorilla being pushed into a police car.

'Well, that's the end of the party,' says Cleopatra.

'I'll give you a lift home,' Dracula says to you.

▪ ■ ▪

You get into Dracula's car and he takes you to your bed and breakfast. You say goodbye to Dracula and you ring the doorbell. The door is opened by Mr Lovedale. 'Oh my God!' he says, holding his chest.

'Sorry, Mr Lovedale, it's only me. I've been to a fancy dress party,' you say.

'What a shock!' says Mr Lovedale. 'I thought my time had come.'

▪ ■ ▪

It is Saturday morning. You are going to catch your plane at two o'clock this afternoon and you do not know what to do about Tom. Sadly, you pack your bags. There is a knock on your door. 'It's your friend Tom on the phone,' says Mrs Lovedale.

You run to the hall and pick up the phone. 'Are you all right? What happened?' you ask.

'Yes, I'm OK,' says Tom. 'The policewoman was a bit angry, but she calmed down after a while, and they took me home. We can meet up later if you like.'

'Great,' you say, 'let's meet at the restaurant in St James's Park at ten o'clock.'

You sit down and eat an English breakfast without any difficulty, impressing the Spaniard sitting next to you. Then you get your bags and you say goodbye to the Lovedales and the two budgerigars - Mr Lovedale has caught Joey (the bird you lost). You take the bus to St James's Park.

You meet Tom at the restaurant in St James's Park and have your last cup of English tea together. 'Come and visit me in Australia,' he says.

'I will, and you must visit me,' you say.

'Well, I'm going to Scotland next week,' says Tom. 'I could visit you after that.'

'Great,' you say. You give him your angel costume and harp. 'Would you mind taking my costume back to the shop?' you ask.

'Not at all,' he says. 'I'm going to wear a policeman's costume at the fancy dress party tonight.'

You promise to write to each other. Sadly (but not too sadly as it is now raining), you take your very heavy bags into the underground station and catch the train to Heathrow Airport.

Two hours later, your plane is flying over London, but unfortunately you cannot see any of the sights as everything is covered in cloud.

Go to section 107 ▶

Section 46 (33)

Answer: d is false.

Win 10 points if you were correct.

The United Kingdom has a very different electoral system from the rest of Europe. The UK is divided into districts called constituencies. In an election, the candidate with the most votes in each constituency wins a seat in the House of Commons and represents his or her constituency.

You leave the Houses of Parliament.

Go to section 89 ▶

Section 47 (35)

The correct order is: c, f, b, d, g, a, e.

Win 10 points if ALL the sentences are in the correct order. (Write down your score.)

You close the door and fall onto the bed. You are tired, but you are happy.

▪ ■ ▪

It is Monday morning. You go down to the dining room for breakfast.

'Good morning,' says Mrs Lovedale. She is short with long, straight brown hair. 'What can I get you?' she asks.

'Just coffee and toast, please,' you say.

'White or black?'

'Toast!?'

'No, coffee. White or black coffee. With or without

milk?' asks Mrs Lovedale.

'White coffee, please.'

You sit next to a friendly American couple. They tell you about their life in the Rocky Mountains, and about their children, and their friends, and their hobbies, and their family, and their car, and their dog, Billy, ... When breakfast is finished, you have a bit of a headache.

Go to section 40 ◀

48

Section 48 (57)

You walk away to find a seat. 'Excuse me!' says the barman. His face is a little redder. 'That's £5.60.'

Lose ② *points.*

Go to section 69 ▶

49

Section 49 (43)

You are lost and you are wasting time.

Lose ⑤ *points.*

You ask a man, 'Excuse me, is there a pet shop near here?'

'Yes, I bought my pet hamster, Timmy, there,' says the man. 'Let me see. Go down this road until you see some traffic lights. Carry on until you come to a hospital. Then turn left. When you come to the end of the road, turn left and it's on your left.'

Go back to section 43 and try again ◀

Section 50 (71)

The correct order is: c, b, f, a, e, d.

Win 10 *points if* ALL *the sentences are in the correct order.*

You pay and take a seat on the top of a red sightseeing* bus. The bus visits all the important sights of London.

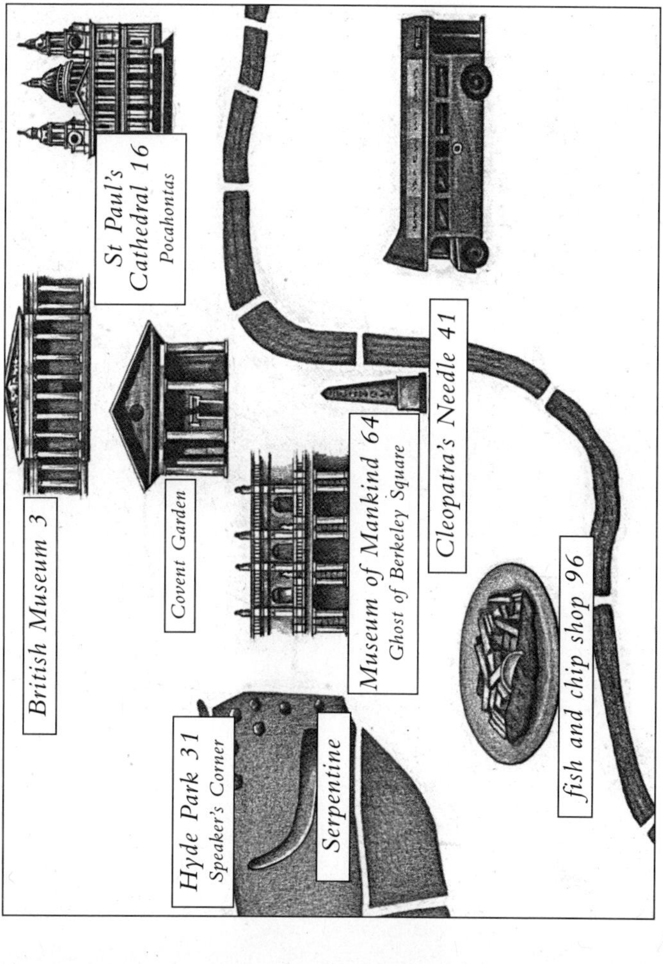

You can use your ticket to get on and off the bus as many times as you want in the same day. There is a guide on the bus who tells you about the sights.

You spend the day visiting different places. Look back at the map on page 55 and visit two or more places. (If you want to go to the Museum of Mankind, for example, go to section 64. If you want to go to the British Museum, go to section 3, and so on. When you have visited enough places, go to section 90.)

Go to section 90 ▶

51

Section 51 (21)

Thirty minutes later, the taxi stops outside a hotel called the 'Crescent Hotel'.

'Here you are,' says the taxi driver. 'That's £36.' You give him a £4 tip*. (It's normal to tip taxi drivers about 10%.) You feel happy that you have found a hotel. The taxi driver looks very happy, too. Heathrow is a long way from the centre of London and the trip was quite expensive. By underground it costs about £4.

Lose (5) points.

(You now have 100 - 5 = 95 points. Write '95' on a piece of paper.)

Go to section 54 ▶

52

Section 52 (73)

You travel to Notting Hill Gate and get onto a District Line southbound train. Twenty minutes later, your train comes out of the tunnel and you pass buildings and the back gardens of houses. The train stops at East Putney. You look at the map and realize that you are in the wrong part of London. You get off the train and take the next train back. You waste half an hour.

Go to section 104 ▶

Section 53 (31)

Incorrect. You are too formal and you sound unfriendly.

Lose ③ ***points.***

Tom starts rowing angrily and splashes you with water. You say, 'Would you mind not splashing me with water?'

Go to section 65 ▶

Section 54 (30) (51)

You go into the hotel. Below is your conversation with the sleepy receptionist. Put the sentences in the correct order.

Example: 1c

a 'With or without bathroom?'
b 'I'm afraid not. You have to pay extra for breakfast.'
c 'I'd like a single room, please.'
d '£80 a night.'
e 'Does that include breakfast?'
f 'With, please. How much is it?'

Go to section 5 ◀

55

Section 55

(32)

Tom thinks you are surprised about something. You shouldn't say 'Jesus' unless you are talking about the real Jesus. Some people may be offended by it.

Lose (3) *points.*

Go back to section 32 and try again ◀|

56

Section 56

(98)

Answers: 1 toothpaste, 2 comb, 3 plaster, 4 needle, 5 soap, 6 thread, 7 socks, 8 a roll of film.

Win (1) *point for* EACH *correct word.*

What things from the list above can you get from a chemist's*? Write them down.

Go to section 81 |▶

57

Section 57

(85) (95)

You have to order at the bar in pubs in Britain. You go to the bar and say, 'Can I have a beer, please?' The barman has served a lot of foreigners today who have never been to an English pub before. He is big with red hair and a red beard. His face is a little red, too. Pointing a fat finger at a large number of bottles and beer taps, he asks, 'Which beer?' (There are many different kinds of beer in England. Foreigners usually drink lager.)

You say, 'I think I'll have a lemonade instead and ...' – you look at the menu – 'a lasagne and salad, please.'

'With or without chips?' asks the barman.
'Without, please.'

What do you do?

- **Pay now.**
  Go to section 69 ▶

- **Pay later when you leave the pub.**
  Go to section 48 ◀

Section 58 (43)

58

Correct. You see a bored cat and a sleepy parrot* in a shop window. You go into the pet shop. Here is your conversation with the shop assistant. Choose one word from the list to complete each space:

after one 'll same for ones like 'd

You: I'm looking (a)... a blue budgerigar.
Assistant: Here are some lovely (b)....
You: Ah, this one looks (c)... Mrs Lovedale's bird. How much is it?
Assistant: £7.
You: I (d)... take it.

Now go to section 80 ▶

Section 59 (81)

59

Correct. 'I've been here for three days,' says Tom.
'How long are you here for?' Tom asks.
'Six days,' you say. 'I'm leaving next Saturday.'

> When you want to talk about an action that begins in the past and continues to the present, you use the present perfect tense (eg *I have lived* ...) or the present perfect continuous tense (eg *I have been living* ...).

During the evening you ask Tom a lot of questions. Complete the questions below. Use *one* word only for each question.

You: What do you (a)...?

Tom: I'm a student.

You: What (b)... of music do you like?

Tom: Rock.

You: Have you (c)... to the Tower of London?

Tom: Yes, I have. I went there two days ago.

You: Have you (d)... eaten Spanish food?

Tom: No, never.

You: Where are you (e)...?

Tom: At the youth hostel near St Paul's Cathedral.

You: What's the hostel (f)...?

Tom: Really good for the price. I've got my own room and you get a big breakfast. Do you always ask so many questions?

Now go to section 106 ▶

Section 60 (44)

The correct order is: b, e, d, a, c.

Win 10 *points if* ALL *the sentences are in the correct order.*

Medical treatment

If you are from a European Community country, you do not have to pay to go to hospital or to see a doctor in Britain. People from all countries can get free emergency treatment.

The cyclist does not look very happy with you. Her red hair is very untidy and she has a plaster on her face.

What do you say?

- **'Aren't you going to say you're sorry?'**
  Go to section 9 ◀❙
- **'I'm terribly sorry. Can I give you a lift home in the taxi?'**
  Go to section 37 ◀❙

Section 61 (42)

You pay and enter a crowded hall. At the end of the hall the Tomcats are playing very loudly. You try to speak to Tom, but he cannot understand you. It is not a good place to practise your English. The music is so loud that your chest* vibrates, and there is so much smoke that your eyes hurt. You are thirsty, but it is impossible to get a drink as there are too many people around the bar.

When you leave two hours later, you are tired, your ears are ringing and your clothes smell of smoke. 'That was great!' shouts Tom.

You get a taxi. 'I'll walk home,' says Tom. You agree to meet tomorrow at the lions in Trafalgar Square.

Go to section 70 ❙▶

62

Section 62

(106)

The lady moves and looks at you angrily.

Incorrect. Lose 3 points.

Go back to section 106 and try again ▶

63

Section 63

(73)

Correct. Win 5 points.

You enjoy looking at the people who get on the train. There are all types of people from all over the world. Some of them are very normal and some are very strange. But you do not see anyone wearing a bowler hat.

Go to section 104 ▶

64

Section 64

(50)

You get off near Piccadilly Circus and walk to the Museum of Mankind in Burlington Gardens (entrance free). The Museum of Mankind is about societies and cultures of the world.

As you go in, you see a group of people at the end of the gallery playing songs and dancing. They are the Kaluli people who live in the forests of Papua New Guinea. Their music imitates the birds, wind, rain and insects of the forest. You see a real house from Papua New Guinea and an exhibition which tells you about their traditions and customs.

Here are some facts about the peoples of the world. *One* of them is false. Which one do you think is false?

a On Lake Titicaca in Bolivia, people live on islands made of reeds (a type of grass that grows in water).

b A thousand years ago in China, some women invented their own language so that men could not understand them. This language still survives today.

c Gypsies* originated in Egypt.

d Some groups of Inuit (Eskimos) control conflicts between two people with 'song fights'. Instead of fighting, enemies have to sing insults. The person who sings better is the winner, and the loser often has to leave the community.

e Easter Island is in the middle of the Pacific Ocean, thousands of kilometres from the nearest inhabited island, but two different races of people arrived there hundreds of years before it was discovered by Europeans.

Go to section 79 ▶

Section 65

(31) (53)

'All right,' says Tom.

> *'Would you mind (not) ...ing?'* is a polite way of asking people to do or not to do things.

Tom rows very quickly. He goes near some young people in another boat. 'Let's have some fun,' he says and he splashes* them.

When you take the boat back, your clothes are completely wet. You are angry with Tom.

You catch the bus at Hyde Park Corner.

Go back to section 50 and visit another place ◀

66

Section 66 (76)

Tom says, 'You look ridiculous, too.'

Go to section 100 ▶

67

Section 67 (69)

The word 'pub' means 'public house'.

There are sometimes two bars in a British pub: the public bar and the lounge or saloon bar. The public bar is often cheaper, but less comfortable, and you can play games there such as darts and dominoes. Some pubs have family rooms where children are allowed.

All ages go to pubs in Britain. In a typical bar in the evening, you can see 20-year-olds and 60-year-olds.

You have to be over 18 to be served in a pub.

All pubs in England must close at 11 o'clock in the evening. In Scotland they can close when they want. Many pubs close in the afternoon from 2.30 to 5.30.

The Tiger Tavern

Near the Tower of London there is a pub called the 'Tiger Tavern'. There is a story that a tunnel once connected the pub to the Tower of London, and that Princess Elizabeth, (later Queen Elizabeth I, 1558-1603), used to go through the tunnel to the pub for a drink. In the pub, you can still see the cat (now in a glass box) that she used to play with when she was having a drink.

Pubs always have a painted sign outside with a picture. Match these pub signs with the names below.

1

2

3

4

5

6

The Lamb and Flag, The Swan, The Bell, The Crown, The Pig and Whistle, The Ship.

Now go to section 77 ▶

68

Section 68

(43)

You cannot find a pet shop. You are lost.

Lose ⑤ *points.*

You ask a lady. 'Excuse me, I have to find a pet shop quickly. Is there one near here?'

The woman looks at the bird cage, then she looks at you. She thinks you are mad and does not say anything. Go back to the Lovedales' bed and breakfast (section 43) and try again.

Go to section 43 ◀|

69

Section 69

(48) (57)

You give the man the money and look for a place to sit down. In pubs you pay at the bar when you order food or drink.

It is sunny now and you have your lunch in a small garden at the back of the pub. The garden is pretty with flowers, wooden tables and benches.

Do you want to know more about British pubs?

- **Yes.** Go to section 67 ◀|
- **No.** Go to section 98 |▶

70

Section 70

(61) (75)

It is Thursday morning. You are surprised to find an English couple sitting next to you. You ask them what they are doing in London and they say that they are tourists, too.

Mr Lovedale sits down and has a cup of tea with you. Sometimes you find it difficult to understand him. He tells you he speaks with a Cockney accent.

The famous Cockney dialect originates from the East End of London. Some Londoners speak with a strong accent and sometimes use 'rhyming slang'. When two words rhyme, they have a similar sound, for example 'meat' rhymes with 'feet'. 'Plates of meat' is Cockney rhyming slang for 'feet'. 'Dog and bone' means 'phone'. ('Bone' rhymes with 'phone'.) However, people use only the first part of the phrase. *For example:* feet = plates of meat = plates

So a Cockney might say, 'My plates are tired. I've been walking all day long.'

Or: phone = dog and bone = dog

So a Cockney might say, 'My mother called me on the dog last night.'

Match the slang phrases with their meanings.

Example: **bacon and eggs – legs**

Slang phrases

bacon and eggs   apples and pears   boat race
brown bread   whistle and flute

Meanings

stairs   face   suit   legs   dead

Go to section 7 ◀▌

Section 71

(106)

Correct. The lady says sorry, too. (English people are sometimes too polite).

> You usually say *'Excuse me'* to attract someone's attention, for example when you want someone to move out of the way or when you are asking directions.
>
> When you want someone to repeat something you have not heard, you can say *'Pardon?'* or *'Sorry?'* with a rising intonation.
>
> When you want to apologize, you normally say *'Sorry'* with a falling intonation.

You leave the underground at Piccadilly Circus and walk to Eros, the famous statue of a little boy with wings in the centre of Piccadilly Circus. The statue is very popular now, but it was a complete disaster for its creator, the sculptor, Sir Arthur Gilbert. The statue cost too much to make and no one liked it when it was first shown in 1893.

There are a lot of people sitting on the steps around the statue, looking at their watches and waiting for people, and it is difficult to find a place to stand. Fortunately, Tom is able to find you. 'I'm sorry I'm late,' he says. 'It's a really nice day and I thought I'd walk here.'

You talk to Tom about what you are going to do today. Put the sentences in the correct order.

a 'We could take one of those buses that shows you sights* of London. The sun is out.'

b 'How about Madame Tussaud's, the waxworks* museum?'

c 'Where shall we go?'

d 'Here at Piccadilly Circus.'

e 'That sounds like a good idea. Where do we catch the bus?'

f 'No, I don't fancy that. There's always a long queue outside the museum.'

Go to section 50

Section 72 (40)

Correct. Win **5** *points.*

The assistant smiles and gives you the umbrella.

Go to section 73

Section 73 (72) (86)

> You say *'Can I have …?'* or *'Could I have …?'* when you want people to give you things.

You walk for a while, looking at the shops. Finally, you find an underground station and ask the ticket clerk.

'Can I have a Weekly Travelcard for Zones 1,2 and 3, please?' (With this card, you can go anywhere in the centre of London by bus or underground for a week.)

'Have you got a photo?' asks the clerk.

Fortunately, you find a very old, dirty photograph of yourself in your bag. You pay for the Travelcard and look at the map of the underground.

The London Underground Map

The London Underground Map is very famous and it is considered to be a triumph of graphic design. The map represents simply and attractively one of the most complicated underground systems in the world. The map was made by Henry Beck in 1931, and the design has now been copied by most of the world's 80 underground systems.

Look at the map of the underground. You are at Lancaster Gate and you want to go to Tower Hill. Which way do you go? *(You will win points if you are correct.)*

- **Take the Central Line westbound to Notting Hill Gate. Change to the District Line southbound.**
  Go to section 52 ◀I
- **Take the Central Line eastbound to Liverpool Street. Change to the Circle Line.**
  Go to section 63 ◀I

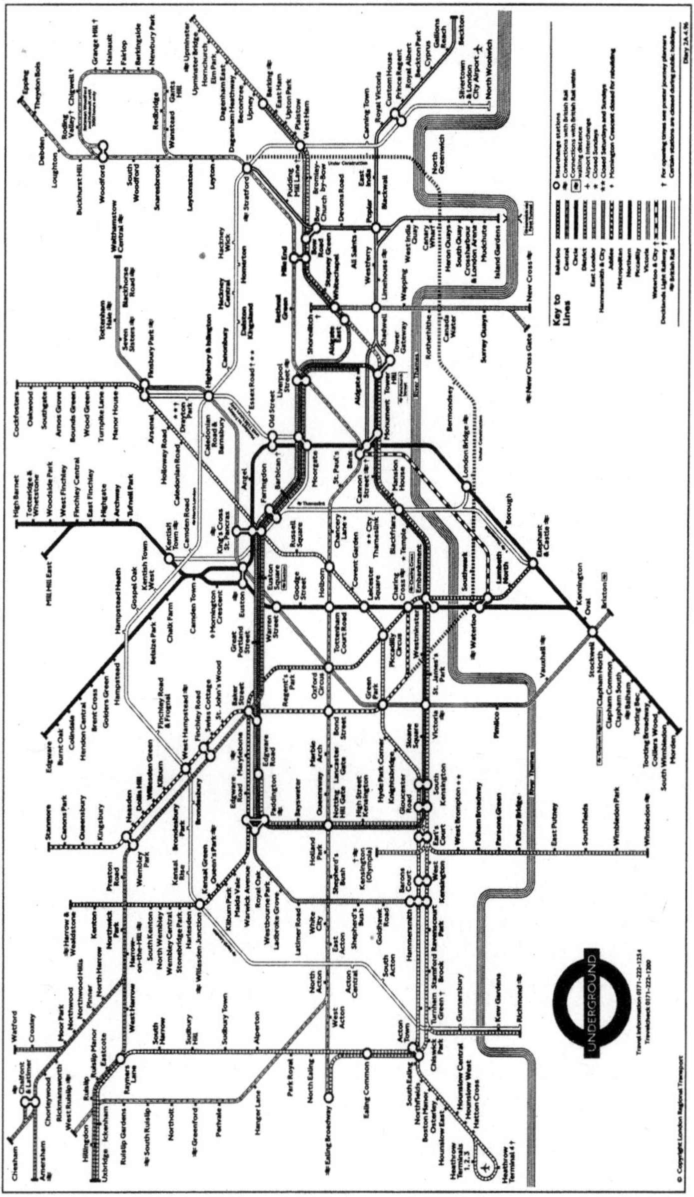

LRT Regd. User No 97/2598

Section 74

(22)

You enter the nave of Westminster Abbey. There has been a church on this site since the seventh century, but most of Westminster Abbey was built in medieval times.

You pay and go into the Royal Chapel. Everywhere are the tombs of kings and queens and memorials to famous British people.

You go into the Chapel of St Edward the Confessor. Edward was the son of King Ethelred, who died in exile in 1016. Edward was a very religious man. He was offered the crown of England in 1042 and, although he preferred life as a scholar, he agreed to become king. While he was king, he spent much of his time building Westminster Abbey. It was completed in 1065, but Edward was too ill to go to the first service there in 1066 and he died a week later. His tomb was very important in medieval times. Even the dust from the area around his tomb was considered sacred.

Opposite the tomb of Edward the Confessor is the tomb of Eleanor of Aquitaine (1122-1204). She was married first to the King of France and later to the King of England. She established 'courts of love' where abstract love problems were discussed.

Also in the Chapel of Edward the Confessor you can see the Coronation* Chair. It has been used at the coronation of every king and queen of England since 1308. Many people have written things on the chair. One message says that a boy slept there all night in 1800.

How much British history do you know? Answer these questions.

1 The Anglo-Saxons invaded England in the fifth century. Where did they come from?
  a France **b** Germany
2 The last people to conquer England were the Normans in 1066. What language did they speak?
  a French **b** German **c** English
3 England had a series of civil wars in the fifteenth century. What were they called?
  a The Wars of the Roses **b** The Wars of the Castles
4 One famous English King had six wives. What was his name?
  a James VI **b** Henry VIII
5 Queen Victoria was a very famous English Queen. In which century did Queen Victoria live?
  a In the eighteenth century **b** In the nineteenth century

Go to section 88 ▶

Section 75 (42)

After dinner, you walk to the Albert Hall near Kensington Gardens. The Henry Wood Promenade Concerts (the 'Proms') are classical music concerts which are held here every year from mid-July to mid-September. They are popular with young people.

You pay and go into the impressive Victorian building, built in 1871, with its high glass dome. Unfortunately, you arrive late and get bad seats high up. The orchestra looks very small.

When the concert ends, you wake Tom up and leave.

You agree to meet tomorrow at the lions in Trafalgar Square. You take a bus home.

Go to section 70 ◀

76

Section 76 (26)

Answers: a about, b suit, c changing, d fit, e size, f take.

Win (2) points for EACH correct answer.

Tom has hired a gorilla costume. He asks, 'What do you think of it?' You think he looks silly.

What do you say?

- **'You look ridiculous.'**
  Go to section 66 ◀
- **'You look good.'**
  Go to section 102 ▶

77

Section 77 (67)

Answers: 1 The Pig and Whistle, 2 The Bell, 3 The Lamb and Flag, 4 The Swan, 5 The Crown, 6 The Ship.

Win (1) point for EACH correct answer.

Go to section 98 ▶

78

Section 78 (90)

'Pardon?' says Tom. He does not understand you.

Incorrect. Lose (5) points.

Go back to section 90 and ask again ▶

Section 79 (64)

Answer: c is false. Gypsies originated in India.

Win 10 points if you answered correctly.

You leave the Museum of Mankind and walk to Berkeley Square.

The True Story of the Ghost of 50 Berkeley Square

It is said that more people have seen ghosts in London than any other city in the world. One of the most frightening of these stories took place at 50 Berkeley Square in the nineteenth century.

One of the ghost's first victims was an English aristocrat, Sir Robert Warboys. After hearing stories about a ghost at 50 Berkeley Square, Sir Robert said he did not believe them and decided to spend a night in the house. The nervous landlord* told Sir Robert to ring a bell if he saw anything unusual, but Sir Robert told the landlord not to worry. At midnight the landlord heard the bell and he ran to the room. Sir Robert was dead. He had died of fright.

Many more people were victims of the ghost until Lord Lyttleton, the celebrated ghost hunter, decided to investigate. He filled a gun with silver coins* and went into the room at night. When he saw a dark shape, Lord Lyttleton fired his gun at it. The ghost disappeared and has never been seen again.

Go to section 50

Section 80

(58)

Answers: a for, b ones, c like, d 'll.

Win 2 points for EACH correct answer.

You pay the assistant, put the bird in the cage and then run back to the house.

Mrs Lovedale comes home ten minutes later while you are sitting reading a book. She stops and looks at the bird in the cage for a long time. 'That's very strange,' she says, 'I've just seen another bird like Joey outside.' You drop your book on the floor. 'But I knew it wasn't Joey,' she says, smiling. 'I know my Joey.' You close your eyes and smile, too.

▪■▪

You take the bus to Piccadilly Circus and meet Tom at the statue of Eros. 'What have you been doing today?' you ask.

'Looking in bookshops in Charing Cross Road,' says Tom. 'I met some really nice Canadians there that I'd met in Egypt a month ago. It's funny - when you are travelling, you meet the same people again and again. What about you? Have you had a good rest?'

'No,' you say and you tell him about Mrs Lovedale's bird.

Tom tells you that budgerigars come from Australia and he tells you where the birds live and what they eat.

It's lunchtime and you walk until you find a pub. Outside there is a sign saying, 'Real Home-made English Food'. When you ask for the menu, the South African barman points to a blackboard on the wall and says that they only have ploughman's lunch and shepherd's pie.

Which do you choose?

- **ploughman's lunch**
  Go to section 87 ▶
- **shepherd's pie**
  Go to section 92 ▶

Section 81 (56)

Answers: plasters, comb, soap, roll of film.

Win 1 point for EACH correct answer.

In some large chemist's you can also get socks.

You want to buy some presents, too, so you take the underground to Oxford Circus. Normally shops close at 5.30 in Britain, but in Oxford Street many shops are open until 6 or 7pm and even later on Thursdays.

After shopping, you look for a place to eat. You pass a Chinese restaurant, an African restaurant, a French restaurant, a Hungarian restaurant ... but you cannot find an English restaurant. Finally you go into an Indian restaurant. It is dark inside and there are pictures of India on the walls.

The waiter gives you the menu, but you do not know what to order. There is a man with brown hair sitting next to you. He is speaking to a waiter. 'Could I have a beef* curry, please?' he asks.

'Hot, medium or mild?' asks the waiter.

'Hot, please,' says the man.

You decide to order a mild beef curry.

Five minutes later, the food arrives and you try the curry. It burns your mouth and you feel very hot. You watch the man calmly eat his hot curry. But after a few minutes, he stops eating. His face goes very red and he drinks a lot of water.

'Good curry, isn't it?' the man says to you after a while.

'Yes,' you say.

You begin talking to each other. His name is Tom and he is from Australia. 'What are you doing in England?' you ask.

'I'm travelling around the world,' he says.

You want to know when he came to Britain.

What do you say?

- **'How long have you been here?'**
  Go to section 59 ◀▌
- **'How long are you here for?'**
  Go to section 91 ▌▶

Section 82 (104)

Answer: 'I'm sorry, I didn't catch what you said. Could you say that again?'

Win 5 points if ALL *the words are in the correct order.*

The yeoman warder says that the birds are called 'ravens'. It is said that if the ravens ever leave the Tower, England will be conquered. The ravens' wings have been cut, so that they cannot escape. They have a keeper who looks after them, and there is a special cemetery for the birds.

You tip the yeoman warder and go into the Jewel House where you can see the Crown* Jewels*. One of the jewels, the Star of Africa, is the largest diamond in the world.

Only one man has ever tried to steal the Crown Jewels. His name was Thomas Blood. Below is the true story of Thomas Blood. Read the story and then put the pictures in the correct order. *Example:* ***1b.***

Thomas Blood was an Irishman who owned a lot of land in Ireland. When Charles II became King in 1660, he took Blood's land from him, and Blood became very angry and bitter.

In 1671 Blood decided to steal the Crown Jewels. He and his wife went to the Tower of London and asked to see the Crown Jewels. The jewels were guarded by a man called Talbot Edwards who made money showing them to people. The Bloods became friends of Mr Edwards and his wife, and they visited them often. The Edwards were worried because their daughter was getting old and she was not married.

a

b

c

d

e

f

Blood said he had a nephew who was looking for a wife, and he would bring him to the Tower to meet their daughter.

One day soon after, Blood came to the Tower early with some friends and his 'nephew'. When Edwards opened the door, Blood attacked him.

By chance, Edwards's son was going to the Tower to visit his father that morning. He discovered Blood and his friends stealing the jewels. Soon the Tower was filled with shouts of 'Robbers!'

One of Blood's friends was captured by a guard. Another robber escaped from the castle, but he hit his head on a shop sign and fell off his horse. After a long fight, Blood was captured by an officer called Captain Beekman.

When the King heard what had happened, he went to the Tower to see Blood. He was impressed by Blood's courage and he pardoned him and gave him back his land in Ireland. Thomas Blood was an influential person in the court of Charles II until his death in 1680.

Go to section 95 ▶

Section 83 (99)

'The man shouts, "No, no! I've already given you some money."'

The MacKennas play a few more songs and everyone sings with them. People are becoming more friendly in the bar. But when everyone is enjoying themselves the most, the lights go on and the barman shouts, 'Time, ladies and gentlemen, please!' It is 11 o'clock, closing time - time to go home.

■ ■ ■

It is Wednesday morning and you walk slowly into the dining room. You sit down carefully at the table. The American gentleman sits next to you saying, 'Hi, how are you doing?'

'Not too well,' you say. 'I ate a hot dog last night and I think it's upset my stomach.'

The American tells you about all the different types of food he has tried from different places in the world. When his English breakfast arrives you say, 'Excuse me,' and go to your room.

You decide to stay in your room this morning. But you need to phone Tom and tell him you cannot meet him. You want to ask Mrs Lovedale if you can use the phone. What do you say to Mrs Lovedale? Put these words in the correct order.

'your mind I use phone you if do?'

Go to section 103 ▶

84

Section 84

(106)

The lady says angrily, 'I didn't say anything!'

Lose 3 points.

Go back to section 106 and try again ▶

85

Section 85

(95)

You wait for five minutes, but nobody comes to serve you.

Lose ② *points.*

Go to section 57 ◀|

Section 86 (40)

Incorrect. The assistant looks at you angrily and then she gives you the umbrella. You are impolite.
You don't win any points.

Go to section 73 ◀|

Section 87 (80)

The barman gives you French bread, butter, tomato, cheese and pickle on the same plate. 'Pickle' is made from pieces of vegetable or fruit preserved in vinegar and sugar.

Go to section 97 |▶

Section 88 (74)

Answers: 1b.

2a The Normans spoke French in the King's court in England for more than 300 years and there are thousands of French words in the English language, eg *royal* comes from old French *roial.*

3a The Wars of the Roses (1455-1485) were fought between the House of Lancaster (red rose) and the House of York (white rose). Nearly all the nobility of England were killed in these wars.

4b English schoolchildren have a rhyme to help them remember what happened to Henry's six wives:

Divorced, beheaded, died,
Divorced, beheaded, survived.

5b Queen Victoria ruled for 63 years. Her rule was known as the Victorian age and it was a very prosperous time for Britain. Her family were German and she never spoke English perfectly.

Win **2** *points for* EACH *correct answer.*

You leave the Chapel and see people rubbing* pieces of gold wax on pieces of black paper. They are doing a brass rubbing – making a copy of the metal surface of an old tomb.

A brass rubbing of a tomb in Westminster Abbey.

'Shall we try?' you ask Tom.

'OK,' says Tom.

You both buy some wax and paper. But it is not as easy as it looks. Eventually you produce two copies to put on your walls at home. You leave Westminster Abbey. Tom's clothes are covered in gold coloured wax.

Go to section 89 ▶

Section 89

(46) (88)

You walk along a wide street called Whitehall, where there are many government offices. You pass Downing Street, where the Prime Minister lives. It is a small street and you are not allowed to enter it.

You walk a little further along Whitehall until you come to the entrance to Horse Guards (the head offices of the Army), where you see two soldiers on horses. You go in and, under an arch, you see a soldier in a black uniform holding a sword. He is standing very still.

Do you ask Tom to take a photo of you standing next to the soldier?

- **Yes.** Go to section 101 ▶
- **No.** Go to section 94 ▶

Section 90

(50)

You and Tom are very hungry after a day of sightseeing. You see a Greek restaurant. 'Let's try some Greek food,' says Tom. Tom tells you that his best friend is Greek and that there are lots of Greeks in Australia. He tries to speak to the waiter in Greek, but the waiter doesn't understand him. The waiter is from Ireland.

When you leave the restaurant, you see a pub on the opposite side of the road. Outside the pub there is a sign saying, 'Folk Night. Guest Singers: The MacKennas.' You want to hear some folk music.

What do you say to Tom?

- **'Shall we go in?'**
  Go to section 99 ▶

- **'Will we go in?'**
  Go to section 78 ◀

91

Section 91

(81)

Tom says, 'I'm going to stay another week in London.' (He thinks you are talking about the future.)

Lose (5) *points.*

Go back to section 81 and ask again ◀

92

Section 92

(80)

Shepherd's pie is made of minced meat and onions, and covered with mashed potatoes. 'Minced' meat is meat that has been cut into very small pieces. Mashed potatoes are potatoes that have been made soft like a purée and mixed with butter and milk.

Go to section 97 ▶

93

Section 93

(103)

Mr Lovedale looks up. 'What's our bird doing up there?' he asks. Your face goes red and you say, 'Yes, I thought it was strange, too.' Mr Lovedale looks at you very hard. He does not believe you.

Lose (5) *points.*

Go to section 43 ◀

Section 94

(89) (101)

You walk to the end of Whitehall and cross the Strand. Opposite Charing Cross Station is Coutts and Co, the Queen's private bank. Until 1993, letters were carried between the bank and Buckingham Palace by horse and carriage*. But as traffic increased, the carriage had more and more collisions with cars, and the custom was stopped. Recently, the bank opened 3,500 deposit boxes in the vaults* that people had left a long time before and had not collected. They found lots of gold, silver, jewels, papers, letters and a beautiful guitar that was left in 1812.

The Bank of England is in the City of London - the financial part of London. England's gold is kept in its vaults, which go three floors under the ground. It has one of the most sophisticated security systems in the world and the vaults fill with water if anyone without authority tries to enter.

Below is a true story about the Bank of England. Use these words to complete the text:

were could received waited checked found

One day the Directors of the Bank of England (a)... a large packet in the post. In the packet were some documents and a note, 'I took these documents from your vaults,' read the note. 'If you want to know how I did it, wait for me in the vaults tonight at midnight.'

The directors (b)... not believe that anyone could get into the vaults of the Bank of England and they thought it was a joke. But they (c)... the documents and they found that they were authentic.

That night the directors and a large number of police

officers (d)... in the vaults. At midnight they heard the sound of stone moving, and they (e)... surprised to see a man appear from the room where the gold was kept. He said he was a tosher. A 'tosher' is a person who explores sewers* and tunnels, looking for jewellery and things of value. One night when he was exploring an old sewer, he moved a large stone and (f)... himself in the Bank of England.

The directors rewarded the tosher well for his honesty; he could have stolen a lot of gold.

Now go to section 105 ▶

95

Section 95

(82)

The correct order is: 2d, 3e, 4f, 5a, 6c.

Win 10 *points if* ALL *the pictures are in the correct order.*

You leave the Tower of London and go to the River Thames where you see the famous Tower Bridge (built in 1894). Everybody thinks it is called London Bridge. The old London Bridge was bought by an American and is now in Lake Havasu City, Arizona, USA. The new London Bridge is the next bridge along the river. There is a museum in Tower Bridge and you can walk along the top of the bridge.

It is lunchtime and you walk along a street looking for a restaurant. You see a sign outside an old pub that says 'Food Now Being Served'. A pub is a good place to have a cheap meal.

You go into the pub. Inside it is dark. The walls are covered with dark wood and metal ornaments.

What do you do?

- **Sit down and wait for someone to serve you.**
  Go to section 85 ◀|
- **Go to the bar and order.**
  Go to section 57 ◀|

96

Section 96

(50)

Tom is hungry. You get off the bus, looking for a restaurant. At the end of the street, you can see people coming out of a fish and chip shop, eating chips from a white paper packet. 'How about having some fish and chips,' says Tom. 'I don't want to spend too much money.' You go in and look at the menu.

Today's Menu

		Medium	Large
Cod		£2.70	£3.10
Haddock		£2.70	£3.10
Plaice		£2.90	£3.30
Chicken Pie	£1.90		
Cornish Pasty	£1.70		
Sausages	40p each		
Chips		90p	£1.20

Cod, haddock and plaice are types of fish which are fried in batter made from flour*, water and egg. A Cornish pasty is a type of pie* made with meat and vegetables. (English people eat a lot of pies.)

You have cod and chips. Tom puts salt and vinegar on his fish and chips and you eat them on a bench* outside.

Go back to section 50 ◀

Section 97 (87) (92)

Tom says he wants to go to the Science Museum. After lunch, you take the underground to South Kensington and follow the signs through the tunnel to the Science Museum. You pay and go in.

'I want to go to the Launch Pad Gallery,' says Tom. 'People say it's the best part of the museum. You can touch and play with things.'

You go up to the first floor. The Launch Pad Gallery is full of children turning wheels, putting things together, pressing buttons, hitting each other ....

Tom tries to operate one machine, but it doesn't work. 'If you turn this wheel,' says a small girl, 'then this part goes up, and then you press this button and pull this part and it all turns. It's very easy.'

'Ah, thank you,' says Tom. He tries again, but it doesn't work. Then he tries another machine and that doesn't work either.

'Let's go somewhere else. This is for kids,' says Tom.

There is a lot to see in the museum: model helicopters that you can control, a real aeroplane you can sit in, the first aeroplane to cross the Atlantic,

'Puffing Billy' - the oldest train in the world, a hot air balloon that goes up and down, one of the Apollo Space Capsules that went to the moon....

Many inventions and discoveries had strange beginnings. Can you match the inventions with the descriptions below?

electricity **the vacuum cleaner** **the car**
the yo-yo **sunglasses** **the hot air balloon**

Example: **a the car**

a The government said it was too dangerous and passed a law that a person had to walk in front of it with a red flag.

b They thought it was too dangerous for people, so they put a pig, a duck and hen into it. It went very high and the animals were very frightened.

c He put the pieces of metal onto the legs of a dead frog* and the legs moved. They could not understand how the frog's legs could move if the frog was dead.

d It was used as a weapon for hunting animals.

e They were first used in fifteenth-century China. Judges wore them so that people in the court could not see the expressions on the judges' faces.

f The first machine was not very successful because it blew dust everywhere and made everything dirtier.

Go to section 2 ◀I

98

Section 98

(69) (77)

After your meal, you ask the barman for a coffee. He asks where you are from and you talk to him for a while. You ask him where the best place for shopping is and he tells you that tourists usually go to Oxford Street.

You leave the pub. You need to buy some things which you forgot to bring with you from your country. Do you know what they are called in English? Match the words with the pictures.

plaster thread needle toothpaste socks a roll of film soap comb

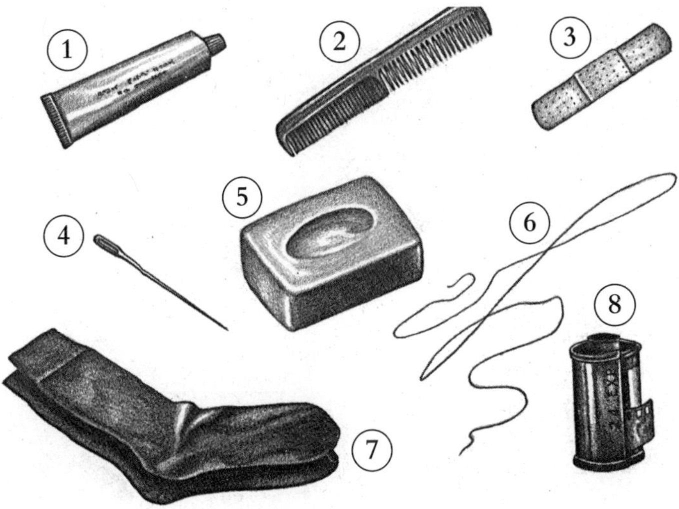

Go to section 56 ◀I

Section 99

(90)

Correct. 'OK' says Tom.

> You can say *'Shall we …?'* to make a suggestion.

Nearly every town in Britain has a folk club – it usually takes place in a pub once a week.

You pay and go in. In the corner there are two chairs and three microphones. A few people from the audience come and sing one or two songs. Some people are good and some are bad, but everyone applauds when they finish.

Finally, the MacKenna Brothers come on. One has a guitar and the other a violin. They play Scottish folk music. Some songs are lively and some are very romantic. The music is similar to Irish music. The words of one of the songs are by the Scottish poet, Robert Burns, and are about a man who has to leave his love and travel to another land.

Besides playing music, the singers usually tell jokes. (Some are better at telling jokes than playing music.) After playing a few songs, one of the MacKennas tells a joke. Do you understand this one?

'A man is walking along the street when he falls down and hurts his leg. Fortunately, two women from the Red Cross are near and they run to help him.

'But when the man sees the women from the Red Cross, he shouts, "No, no! I've already ...."'

Can you guess the end of the joke? What does the man say?

Go to section 83 ◀I

Section 100

(66) (102)

You buy some wine and take a taxi to the party. 'It's the first time I've had an angel and a gorilla in my car,' says the taxi driver. You come to a quiet street and hear African music coming from one of the houses. You have to walk down some steps to the door.

Tom takes off his gorilla mask and rings the bell. A man answers the door. He looks a little surprised when he sees you and Tom. You notice that he is not wearing fancy dress. 'Hello, I'm Janet's friend,' says Tom.

'Come in. She's in the kitchen,' says the man, smiling.

The kitchen is full of people. None of them is wearing fancy dress. 'Why are you wearing that?' asks Janet.

'You told me it was a fancy dress party!' says Tom.

'That's tomorrow night, you idiot!' says Janet, laughing. 'I told you tonight is a normal party and tomorrow is fancy dress. You never listen!'

Everyone is looking at you. Tom puts on his gorilla mask. You don't know what to do. You try to go into the kitchen to get a drink, but you keep hitting people with your wings. 'Go and get me a Coke!' you say to Tom angrily. 'It's all right for you - they can't see your face.'

You go into the large living room where the music is coming from. It is nearly empty. Two girls are dancing. A man is sitting on the sofa with a glass in his hand, looking at the wall. A couple are kissing in the corner. There are some snacks on a table: salads, peanuts, potatoes, garlic bread, pieces of carrot, small pieces of toast. You nervously eat a peanut.

'It's very hot in this suit,' says Tom.

'What are we going to do? I feel like a complete idiot,' you say.

After a few minutes, Janet comes into the room.

'Look,' she says, 'I've got some good news: a friend of mine has got a friend called Jane. Jane knows everyone around this part of London. She says she knows someone who is having a fancy dress party. Why don't you go to that?'

You look at her suspiciously. But Tom says, 'Come on! Let's try it.'

'Wait a minute!' you say. 'I'll go and get my harp. I left it in the kitchen.'

You get in Janet's car and she drives you up the road. Soon you see a Napoleon and a Groucho Marx going into a house.

You get out of the car, say goodbye to Janet and ring the doorbell. Cleopatra answers the door.

'Hello,' says Tom. 'I'm King Kong and this is the Angel Gabriel.'

'Nice to meet you,' says Cleopatra. 'Come in.'

Cleopatra introduces you to everyone. You spend the evening talking to people and dancing. You enjoy yourselves enormously.

Below are Cleopatra's conversations with different people at the party. Who is Cleopatra talking to? Identify the speaker in each conversation.

Example: **a alien**

Dracula Superman clown alien pirate policewoman

Cleopatra: Where are you from?
a: Venus.

Cleopatra: Sorry I stood on your foot.
b: That's OK. I'm invulnerable.

Cleopatra: Would you like a drink?
c: No, thank you. I'm not allowed to drink

when I'm on duty.

Cleopatra: Can I get you anything?

d: Yes, a glass of rum and some nuts for the parrot.

Cleopatra: Can't you be serious for one minute!

e: No!

Cleopatra: Can I get you anything to drink?

f: No, I'll help myself, thanks. Let me kiss your neck!

Go to section 45 ◀I

Section 101 (89)

Everyone does that. Poor guard. He does not move or smile for the photograph.

Go to section 94 ◀I

Section 102 (76)

Tom says, 'You look good, too.'

Go to section 100 ◀I

Section 103 (83)

Answer: 'Do you mind if I use your phone?'

Win 5 *points if you put* ALL *words in the correct order.*

'Do you mind if I …?' is a polite way of asking someone if you can do something. (But

intonation is very important in English, and how you say something is often more important than the structure you use.)

Mrs Lovedale says, 'Not at all.' You phone Tom's hostel. Luckily, the person who answers the phone is Tom's friend, Janet, and she finds Tom. You agree to meet Tom in the afternoon.

You decide to spend the morning lying on your bed and watching the television. There is a knock on the door. It is Mrs Lovedale. She says, 'I'm going out. I've got to visit my mother in hospital. Would you mind taking a message for me if anyone phones?'

You say weakly, 'Not at all.'

Half an hour later, when you are watching an interesting programme, the phone rings. You go downstairs and pick up the phone. 'I'm afraid Mrs Lovedale isn't here at the moment,' you say. 'Can I take a message?'

You take the message and when you put the phone down, you hear a bird singing. It is Joey, Mrs Lovedale's blue budgerigar. The bird's food container has fallen down and you open the cage door to put the container back. Joey flies out of the cage into the dining room and then through the window into the garden.

You run out and see the bird in a tree in the front garden. You are climbing the tree when someone shouts, 'Hey! What are you doing up there?' It is Mr Lovedale.

What do you say?

- **'The wind blew a £5 note out of my hand into your tree and I was trying to get it.'**
  Go to section 93 ◀

- **'I'm terribly sorry, but your bird has escaped and I was trying to catch it.'**
  Go to section 43 ◀

Section 104 (52) (63)

When you leave the underground, you can see people queuing in the rain for the Tower of London. In the queue you start talking to an American girl with wet black hair. She says that the weather in America is better than in England, and you say that the weather in your country is better than in England, too. But an Englishman with a white face behind you says that the weather is not always so bad, and that a week ago it was sunny for a whole day.

Finally, you pay and go through the gate* in the castle walls. You are lucky: a guided tour is

beginning. A man wearing fifteenth-century clothes (called a 'yeoman warder' or 'beefeater') takes you to the White Tower and shows you where the prisoners were kept. You see a room full of swords* and other weapons*, and St John's Chapel, the oldest church in England. The yeoman warder takes you to Tower Green and shows you the place where the prisoners' heads were cut off. Then you go to the Bloody Tower where the two sons of King Edward IV were probably murdered.

The yeoman warder points to some fat black birds on the

grass and talks about them, but you do not understand him. You want him to repeat what he said. Look at these two sentences and put the words in the correct order.

you didn't what I sorry I'm said catch.
that again say you could?

Go to section 82 ◀|

Section 105 (94)

***Answers:** a received, b could, c checked, d waited, e were, f found.*

Win 2 points for EACH correct word.

You spend an hour in the National Gallery in Trafalgar Square (entrance free). It has one of the world's best collections of Western European paintings. You see paintings by van Eyck, Rembrandt, Leonardo da Vinci, El Greco. Tom prefers the Impressionist paintings.

You leave the National Gallery and walk to Leicester Square. There are a lot of theatres and cinemas in this area.

'Shall we go to a show tonight?' you ask Tom.

'OK,' says Tom. In Leicester Square there is a kiosk which sells tickets for the theatre. You ask if they have a ticket for the show *Rats* tonight. 'I've only got one ticket left for *Rats*,' says the woman. 'It's the last one. You should buy a ticket a few days before the show if you want to be sure of getting a seat.'

'You take it,' says Tom. 'I'd rather go to a rock concert tonight.'

The woman gives you a standby ticket. Standby tickets are cheaper than normal tickets because they are sold just before the performance* begins.

After eating, you walk to the theatre in Shaftesbury Avenue and take your seat. Soon the curtain goes up and 20 people dressed as rats come onto the stage, singing. When the actors begin to speak, a woman next to you starts talking to her friend.

You want to ask her to stop speaking. Put these sentences in the correct order.

a 'I said "SHE'S A BIT DEAF!"'
b 'Oh, all right.'
c 'Would you mind not speaking? I can't hear the performance.'
d 'Pardon?'
e 'Can't you tell her later?'
f 'Sorry. I'm telling my friend what the people are saying. She can't hear - she's a bit deaf.'

Go to section 44 ◀

Section 106 (59)

Answers: a do, b kind/type, c been, d ever, e staying, f like.

Win 2 points for EACH correct word.

'Maybe I should move to the hostel,' you say.

'It's full,' says Tom. 'You should reserve a place if you want to stay in summer. And you need a Youth Hostel Card. I've got a friend working there - I can ask her, if you like.'

'No, that's OK, thanks,' you say. 'I'll stay where I am.'

Tom tells you about India and Egypt, and other places he has visited. He tells you he went trekking in Nepal.

'What are you studying?' you ask.

'Veterinary medicine. I want to be a vet - you know, an animal doctor,' he says. 'I like animals and I'll be able to get a job in the country going around farms. I don't want to live in a town.'

You enjoy talking to Tom and you agree to meet each other tomorrow at the statue of Eros in Piccadilly Circus. You take a bus home.

▪ ■ ▪

It is Tuesday morning. Through the dining room window, you can see the Lovedales' cats sleeping in the sun. You are sitting next to a French couple who are touring England by car. Speaking quietly, they tell you how strange they think the English are.

Mrs Lovedale comes smiling out of the kitchen. 'Would you like a cooked breakfast this morning?' she asks.

'Yes,' you say bravely, 'I'd like to try an English breakfast.'

Mrs Lovedale brings you a large plate. On it there is: a fried* egg, fried bacon, fried bread, fried black pudding (a sausage* made from pig's blood), a fried sausage and fried tomatoes.

The French couple look at the plate. Then they look at you. 'Are you going to eat it?' asks the man, surprised. You say that if the English can eat it, you can, too. The breakfast will fill you up and you won't have to eat a big lunch. You eat it slowly. The black pudding is surprisingly nice and a little sweet. But you don't know what to think of the sausage. When you have finished your cup of tea, you stand up slowly. Your stomach feels very heavy. You smile weakly at the couple and you go to your room.

You want to rest on your bed, but you have to meet Tom. You go to the underground station and get on a train. The train starts suddenly and you accidentally push an old lady.

What do you say?

- **'Excuse me.'**
  Go to section 62 ◀I
- **'Sorry.'**
  Go to section 71 ◀I
- **'Pardon.'**
  Go to section 84 ◀I

Section 107

Well done. You have come to the end of the story. Did you have a good time in London? Go back to the beginning (section 1) and check your score. Then answer the questions at the back of the book.

EXERCISES

A Comprehension

1 What is the name of the airport where you landed (it is London's main airport)? *Section 10*
2 Do you need a photograph to buy a Weekly Travelcard? *Section 73*
3 What do we call the soldiers who wear sixteenth-century uniform and act as guides at the Tower of London? *Section 104*
4 Thomas Blood tried to steal the Crown Jewels of England, but he was captured. The King visited Thomas Blood in prison. What did the King do to Thomas Blood? *Section 82*
5 What is the name of the famous bridge that crosses the Thames at the Tower of London? *Section 95*
6 When you go to a pub, do you sit down and wait to be served or do you order your drink at the bar? *Section 57*
7 What is the minimum age at which you can be served in a pub? *Section 67*
8 Can you get a roll of film at a chemist's? *Section 81*
9 In the British Museum you can see the Elgin Marbles. Where are the Elgin Marbles from? *Section 20*
10 Where is Speaker's Corner? *Section 31*
11 Where did gypsies originally come from? *Section 79*
12 Who designed St Paul's Cathedral? *Section 16*
13 Did Pocahontas visit London? *Section 36*
14 Where did you buy a new budgerigar for Mrs Lovedale? *Section 58*
15 What did judges wear in fifteenth-century China so that people could not see the expressions on their faces? *Section 2*
16 What idea was inspired by a machine that blew dust everywhere? *Section 2*
17 Did dinosaurs build nests? *Section 17*

....

18 Who was Prince Albert? *Section 32*
19 Name a magazine that tells you what is happening in London. *Section 42*
20 What does 'dog and bone' mean in Cockney rhyming slang? *Section 70*
21 Whose statue can you see in Trafalgar Square? *Section 7*
22 Where does the Queen live? *Section 34*
23 Where are the kings and queens of England crowned? *Section 74*
24 Where do Members of Parliament debate? *Section 33*
25 Where can you buy tickets for musicals and plays? *Section 105*
26 What famous historical figure ordered everyone to drive on the right? *Section 12*
27 Which two universities take part in the famous Boat Race on the Thames every year? *Section 6*
28 Where is there a very famous maze? *Section 28*
29 What did Tom wear to the fancy dress party? *Section 76*
30 Why did Tom leave the fancy dress party? *Section 45*

B Working with Language

1 What would you say in these situations?

a You don't understand what someone says. You want them to repeat what they have just said.
b You want to buy a comb at a chemist's.
c You are at a friend's house. You do not know the friend very well. You want to switch on the television.
d Your friend sneezes.
e You are going out to eat with a friend. You want to have an Indian meal, but you are not sure if your friend likes Indian food.
f You are in a cinema and some people next to you are talking. You can't hear the film.
g You have just met someone at a party. You want to know what their job is.
h A friend has been to Scotland. You want to know if Scotland is beautiful, ugly, clean, expensive, cold, and so on.

i You want to go to the station. You have a heavy suitcase. Your friend has a car.

j You go to a shop and try on a sweater, but you do not think that it goes with your eyes. The assistant wants to know if you want to buy it.

k You want to invite a friend to go out for a Chinese meal.

l You try on another sweater. You like this one. The assistant wants to know what you think.

2 Where would you hear people saying the things below? Choose from this list of places.

underground sightseeing bus Indian restaurant Tower of London pub clothes shop fish and chip shop party hospital chemist's

a 'You can get on and off where you like.'
b 'When is a guided tour beginning?'
c 'Can I get you anything?'
d 'Hot, medium or mild?'
e 'Hold on, I'll put a bandage on it.'
f 'Take the Piccadilly Line westbound.'
g 'It doesn't fit me.'
h 'How much is this comb?'
i 'I'll have a large cod and chips, please.'
j 'I'm sorry, it's eleven o'clock - closing time.'

C Activities

1 Write a letter to your aunt in Australia. Tell her about your trip to London.

2 Your friend is going to London. Give him or her some advice. Make a list of things he or she should do and should not do in London.

3 Make a list of differences between England and your own country.

GLOSSARY

bell *(n)* a metal object that makes a noise when you hit it; a church usually has a *bell* in its tower

beef *(n)* meat from a cow

bench *(n)* a long seat for more than one person

bury *(v)* put someone or something under the ground

carriage *(n)* a wheeled vehicle pulled by a horse

ceiling *(n)* the part of a room above your head

chamber *(n)* a room for debates and large official meetings

chemist's *(n)* pharmacy

chest *(n)* upper part of the front of the body

clown *(n)* someone who wears funny clothes and makes people laugh; the *clowns* in a circus often throw water at each other and at the audience

coin *(n)* a round piece of metal used as money

crown *(n)* what a king or queen wears on their head; *verb* **crown**; *noun* **coronation** the ceremony where the *crown* is symbolically placed on the new king or queen's head

dome *(n)* a hemispherical roof on a church or other building; two buildings in Rome have very famous *domes* - the Pantheon and St Peter's

duck *(n)* small water bird, wild or domestic; can be eaten

earthquake *(n)* sudden escape of energy under the earth's surface causing the earth to move and shake violently

firework *(n)* fireworks provide nighttime outdoor displays of noise and light in the sky

flour *(n)* corn is ground to make *flour*; *flour* is used to make bread

fried *(adj)* *(culinary)* cooked in fat over a high heat

frog *(n)* an amphibious creature with a short tailless body, a wet, smooth skin and strong back legs for jumping long distances

gate *(n)* an outdoor entrance to, for example, a field or other enclosed outdoor space

gypsy *(n)* *gypsies* are a race of people who traditionally live in caravans and move from place to place doing seasonal work

hire *(v)* rent

jewel *(n)* precious stone

landlord *(n)* a man who owns a house or building; **landlady** is the female equivalent

legend *(n)* a popular story from history which may or may not be true

oven *(n)* enclosed part of a cooker

parrot *(n)* large, brightly coloured tropical bird that can be trained to speak; pirates traditionally have *parrots* as pets

pet shop *(n)* shop where domestic animals are sold

performance *(n)* a *performance* is one night of a play, ballet, opera; one night the *performance* might be good, the next night the *performance* might be bad because the actors are tired

pie *(n)* a type of food where meat, fruit or vegetables are cooked in pastry, which is made with flour* and fat

race *(n)* a competition between, for example, runners or cars, to find the quickest

remains *(pl n)* what is left of an old building that has mostly fallen down

ring *(v)* make a noise with a bell*; the telephone *rings* when someone is calling you; you *ring* the doorbell when you want to attract someone's attention

rub *(v)* move one thing over another, applying pressure

row *(n)* move a boat forward with oars (long pieces of wood) and muscle power

sailor *(n)* a person who works on a boat or ship

sauce *(n)* a liquid that is served with a dish to give it more flavour

sausage *(n)* a long, thin roll of meat, for example, a salami

sewer *(n)* a tunnel for carrying dirty water

sight *(n)* a place of interest to tourists; for example, Stonehenge is the most visited *sight* in England; *noun* **sightseeing** means visiting *sights* or places of interest

sink *(v)* a ship *sinks* if it disappears underwater; *past tense* **sank**

sneeze *(v)* suddenly expel air from the nose; you *sneeze* a lot when you have a cold

splash *(v)* to make something wet by throwing water

sword *(n)* a long, thin metal weapon*; King Arthur's famous *sword* was called 'Excalibur'

tip *(n & v)* give someone extra money above the price of the service you have bought from them; for example, you might *tip* a taxi driver by giving him or her 10% extra

vault *(n)* very secure rooms under a bank

waxwork *(n)* statue made from **wax**, a soft modelling material used to make candles

weapon *(n)* something used to fight with

whale *(n)* the largest animal in the world; it lives in the sea

yard *(n)* unit of distance; 1 *yard* = 0.9144 metre

Acknowledgements

The author would like to thank Derek G Peters, City of London Guide and Lecturer, for helping with facts, stories and checking details, Clive Oxenden for his invaluable support and feedback, and all the students who helped to pilot the book.

2005, licensed for:
Bildungshaus Schulbuchverlage
Westermann Schroedel Diesterweg
Schönigh Winklers GmbH
Georg-Westermann-Allee 66
38104 Braunschweig
Germany

Published by Richmond Publishing® 1997
This edition published by Richmond Publishing 2006

ISBN:3-425-71916-5

Cover Design: Giles Davies Design

Cover Illustration: Mac McIntosh

Illustrations: Lee Stannard